PIMPINONE

RECENT RESEARCHES IN THE MUSIC OF THE BAROQUE ERA

Robert L. Marshall, general editor

A-R Editions, Inc., publishes six quarterly series—

Recent Researches in the Music of the Middle Ages and Early Renaissance,
Margaret Bent, general editor;

Recent Researches in the Music of the Renaissance,
James Haar and Howard Mayer Brown, general editors;

Recent Researches in the Music of the Baroque Era,
Robert L. Marshall, general editor;

Recent Researches in the Music of the Classical Era,
Eugene K. Wolf, general editor;

Recent Researches in the Music of the Nineteenth and Early Twentieth Centuries,
Rufus Hallmark, general editor;

Recent Researches in American Music,
H. Wiley Hitchcock, general editor—

which make public music that is being brought to light
in the course of current musicological research.

Each volume in the *Recent Researches* is devoted
to works by a single composer or to a single genre of composition,
chosen because of its potential interest to scholars and performers,
and prepared for publication according to the standards that govern
the making of all reliable historical editions.

Subscribers to this series, as well as patrons of subscribing institutions,
are invited to apply for information about the "Copyright-Sharing Policy"
of A-R Editions, Inc., under which the contents of this volume
may be reproduced free of charge for study or performance.

Correspondence should be addressed:

A-R EDITIONS, INC.
315 West Gorham Street
Madison, Wisconsin 53703

RECENT RESEARCHES IN THE MUSIC OF THE BAROQUE ERA • VOLUME XLIII

Tomaso Albinoni

PIMPINONE

Intermezzi comici musicali

Libretto by Pietro Pariati

Edited by Michael Talbot

A-R EDITIONS, INC. • MADISON

© 1983 by A-R Editions, Inc.
All rights reserved
Printed in the United States of America

Library of Congress Cataloging in Publication Data:

Albinoni, Tomaso, 1671–1750.
    Pimpinone : intermezzi comici musicali.

    (Recent researches in the music of the baroque era,
ISSN 0484-0828 ; v. 43)
    Libretto, with English translation: p.
    Includes bibliographical notes.
    1. Operas—Scores.   2. Operas—Librettos.   I. Pariati,
Pietro, 1665–1733.   II. Talbot, Michael.   III. Albinoni,
Tomaso, 1761-1750.   Pimpinone.   Libretto.   English &
Italian.   1982.   IV. Title.   V. Series: Recent researches
in the music of the baroque era ; v. 43.

M2.R238   vol. 43   [M1500]   82-18420
ISBN 0-89579-169-2

Contents

Preface

Albinoni's *Pimpinone*, published here for the first time in a modern edition, belongs to the genre known as the comic intermezzo. This genre was extraordinarily popular in Italy and in centers of Italian culture during the first half of the eighteenth century, and it was cultivated by many of the most eminent librettists and composers. Although the comic intermezzo cannot be equated with comic opera (see below), its style and mood have much in common with those of the *opera buffa*, and, in certain respects, the intermezzo can be regarded as its precursor.

One of the reasons the repertory of the comic intermezzo is little explored is that not much musical source material has survived. The present setting of *Pimpinone* (libretto by Pietro Pariati) survives complete in a manuscript in the possession of the Österreichische Nationalbibliothek, Vienna; it exists in fragmentary form in the Diözesan-Bibliothek, Münster, and in the Mecklenburgische Landesbibliothek, Schwerin.

The Composer

Tomaso Albinoni, born in Venice on 8 June 1671, was the eldest son of a wealthy paper manufacturer and retailer, Antonio Albinoni (ca. 1634–1709).[1] In his youth Tomaso became a proficient violinist and singer. His first attempts at composition, in the field of church music, were unsuccessful; but an opera, *Zenobia, regina de' Palmireni*, produced in Venice in 1694, and a set of trio sonatas, published there in the same year, ushered in a remarkably long and illustrious career for Albinoni as a composer of secular vocal music (operas, serenatas, and cantatas) and instrumental music (sonatas and concertos). In 1705 Albinoni followed a common practice among Venetian composers of his time by marrying a singer—in Albinoni's case, the soprano Margherita Raimondi (ca. 1684–1721). Until his father's death, he habitually styled himself "dilettante," in acknowledgment of his amateur status; but after the family business passed to two younger brothers, he dropped the epithet. Albinoni is reported to have established in Venice—precisely when is unclear—a successful and profitable school of singing.[2] At no time during his life is he known to have held a regular appointment, although in 1743, when Antonio Pollarolo left the post of *Maestro di coro* at the Ospedaletto, Albinoni was a candidate for that position; however, it was Nicolò Porpora who succeeded Pollarolo.[3] Albinoni paid occasional visits to other cities in connection with productions of his operas (Florence, 1703, and Munich, 1722) and stage appearances of his wife. After a long period of inactivity, he died on 17 January 1751 (1750, Venetian style).[4]

North of the Alps, Albinoni was best known for his instrumental music, the bulk of which is contained in nine collections (opp. 1–3 and 5–10) published between 1694 and 1735/6.[5] The wide dissemination of this music was assisted by the rapid increase (after 1700) in numbers of works that were published by the process of engraving. Chief practitioners of the engraver's art during Albinoni's lifetime were the Amsterdam firm of Estienne Roger (and its successor, the firm of Michel-Charles Le Cène) and the London firm of John Walsh. Concise, tuneful, somewhat restrained in style, and of only moderate technical difficulty, Albinoni's sonatas and concertos suited northern European taste and conditions of performance to perfection. In the first decade of the eighteenth century, before Vivaldi took over the lead, Albinoni's concertos could be rated the most stylistically and formally advanced works in their genre.

In Italy, by contrast, Albinoni was most celebrated for his vocal music; at the most conservative estimate, he composed over fifty operas, an oratorio, three serenatas, over forty cantatas, and three sets of intermezzi.[6] Not until the late 1720s, when Neapolitans were challenging the native Venetians for supremacy as composers for the Venetian stage, did the tempo of Albinoni's operatic production (sustained with remarkable regularity since the 1694 *Zenobia*) slacken; and even so, a flicker of activity persisted until his composition of *Artamene* (1741). Although most of Albinoni's operas were written for the Venetian stage, several were commissioned by opera houses in other Italian cities (Bologna, Brescia, Ferrara, Florence, Genoa, Milan, Piacenza, Rome, and Treviso) and abroad (Munich and Prague). Moreover, the impressive number of eighteenth-century revivals—some supervised by the composer, others mounted independently—confirms Albinoni's position as one of the foremost opera composers working in Venice in the first half of the eighteenth century and identifies him as a worthy rival to Carlo Francesco Pollarolo, Antonio Lotti, Francesco Gasparini, and Antonio Vivaldi. Seeking to account for the success of Albinoni's operas, the historian Francesco Caffi observed that although his style lacked finesse, its robust vigor and popular character appealed to the public.[7]

The Librettist

Pietro Pariati was born on 26 March 1665 in Reggio Emilia, a town in the duchy of Modena.[8] His father, Giovanni Battista Pariati, was a soldier in Modenese service. Pietro studied law and letters in Reggio and graduated "con plauso" in 1687. He then took holy orders and became a secular priest (*abate*), and, in 1695, having already earned a name as a writer of both Italian and Latin lyrics, he was appointed secretary to the governor of Modena. In 1696 he went to Madrid with a special envoy from the duke of Modena; however, Pariati conducted himself so badly there, carrying on amorous intrigues and committing various acts of insubordination, that when he returned to Modena in September 1697, he was dismissed from the duke's service and imprisoned. Released in November 1699, he was sent into permanent exile. He settled in Venice, where he tried to eke out a living by writing. He received generous support from the eminent dramatic poet Apostolo Zeno (1668–1750), with whom he collaborated in the writing of several opera libretti, of which the first was *Artaserse* (1705). The nature of Pariati's contribution to this collaboration is not evident from the libretti themselves, but in a preface to the ninth volume of his *Poesie drammatiche*, Zeno claimed that the subjects and scenarios were his (Zeno's) alone, and that Pariati merely shared the task of putting the dramas into verse.[9] A smaller number of libretti, beginning with *Sidonio* (1706), were written by Pariati alone. By 1708 he was receiving commissions from the Hapsburgs; in that year his "componimento da camera," *Il piú bel nome*, was performed in Barcelona, with music by Caldara, to celebrate the name-day of Elisabeth Christine, wife of the Archduke Charles, who was eventually to become Emperor Charles VI.[10] Other short dramatic works and an oratorio libretto followed. When the post of Second Caesarian Poet became vacant in January 1714 through the death of Pietro Andrea Bernadoni, Emperor Charles VI acted on a recommendation from Zeno and invited Pariati to Vienna, where, in August 1714, he was appointed *kaiserlicher Kammerdichter*. Pariati's main responsibility was the writing of texts for oratorios and for such occasional compositions as serenatas and *feste teatrali*. However, the reluctance of the First Caesarian Poet, Silvio Stampiglia (1664–1725), to serve the new emperor gave Pariati the opportunity to provide libretti for court operas; for some of these opera libretti, Pariati drew on works written earlier for Venetian opera houses, including products of his collaboration with Zeno, such as *Sesostri* (1717).[11] Stampiglia retired to Rome in 1718 and was succeeded by Zeno. Out of deference to his old colleague, Zeno renounced the title of "First" Poet, but his seniority is nevertheless evident from the fact that he took over the major responsibility for opera libretti. After 1718, Pariati remained active as a librettist of *tragicommedie*, writing three further works in this newly fashionable genre and collab-

orating on two more with Zeno. In 1727 another protégé of Zeno, Giovanni Claudio Pasquini, displaced Pariati as principal librettist for oratorios and occasional works; and although Pariati continued to receive his salary, he was not asked to produce any more texts. Pariati died in 1733.[12]

Some fifty dramatic works by Pariati are known. They comprise six *drammi per musica* (ten more were written with Zeno in Venice), four *tragicommedie* (not counting three in collaboration with Zeno), twenty-six occasional works, thirteen oratorios, and the comic intermezzi *Pimpinone*. It is hardly conceivable that he did not write other sets of intermezzi while he was in Venice and perhaps also while he was in Vienna, but because of the difficulty of establishing the authorship of libretti in this genre (see below), we may never know just how many such texts Pariati wrote.[13] His *tragicommedie* demonstrate that he had a marked penchant for comic subjects and that he possessed a gift for satire and the ability to invent sparkling dialogue.[14]

The Comic Intermezzo

Recognition of the comic intermezzo as an important theatrical genre that is entirely distinct from comic opera has come only recently.[15] Around 1700 two originally distinct practices, that of inserting intermezzi (or *intermedii*) of various kinds between operatic acts and that of reserving certain scenes within operatic acts for a pair of comic characters, coalesced to give rise to the comic intermezzo. The convergence of the two practices had been observable for some time before 1700. Charles Troy notes that in Venetian opera of the period between 1650 and 1670, the comic characters, typically an old nursemaid (*vecchia*, often sung as a travesty role by a tenor) and a young manservant (*paggio*, often sung by a female voice), commonly appear in the dramatic action of the opera just before the intermezzo proper.[16] However, the point had not yet been reached (see below) where these characters belong exclusively to the intermezzo. Indeed, in Venetian opera at the close of the seventeenth century, the comic role is more often assigned to a single character, who, except in an occasional monologue, cannot do otherwise than interact with the principal characters in the opera.

In Naples, on the other hand, comic scenes (*scene buffe*) involving two characters who interact with each other flourished within the operas at this time. Such scenes were even added by resident composers to "imported" Venetian operas that already possessed a comic element.[17] But because there were sometimes as many as seven *scene buffe* inserted into one opera, these scenes were not placed as a matter of course in the entr'acte position. Nor did the two comic characters in these scenes relinquish a connection, even if merely formal, with the main plot.

The final stage in the development of the Venetian

comic intermezzo was precipitated by the reform of opera initiated around the turn of the century by Apostolo Zeno and certain other librettists. As a result of that reform, comic scenes were banished from *opera seria*; however, since the public retained its taste for them, they were allowed to find asylum as additional scenes placed between the acts. This placing of comic scenes after the ends of the acts was turned to advantage: the formerly disparate comic scenes could now be welded into an independent dramatic entity; and topical or satirical subjects, not limited by the historical or geographical setting of the opera, could be admitted. Further, since a set of comic intermezzi was no more closely linked with one opera than with another, a given set could be inserted into any work without loss of congruity. The typical combination of a three-act opera with a set of three intermezzi meant that the last intermezzo in a set could not occupy an entr'acte position; therefore, this intermezzo was usually placed mid-way through the third act of the opera, before a change of scenery.[18]

Except for the set of intermezzi for the characters Bleso and Lesba performed at the theater of S. Angelo in 1700, which is an isolated phenomenon, the earliest fully developed Venetian intermezzi were performed in 1706. Between 1706 and 1709, according to Troy, no less than nineteen sets of intermezzi were staged, chiefly at the theater of S. Cassiano.[19] These include the first examples of works belonging to what Troy terms the "international" intermezzo repertory—a nucleus of works that were repeatedly performed all over Italy and in many other European centers. The diffusion of Albinoni's *Pimpinone* followed a typical pattern. From Venice (1708) it spread first to Milan and Naples (1709) and then, between 1710 and 1725, to at least thirteen other Italian centers, metropolitan and provincial. There were performances of *Pimpinone* north of the Alps, in Munich (1722), Brussels (1728), Moscow (1731), and Ljubljana (1740).[20] The fact that *Pimpinone* was performed in Moscow reminds us that the brevity and simplicity of comic intermezzi and the modesty of their demands on vocal, instrumental, and theatrical resources made them ideal vehicles for the advance of Italian opera into hitherto unconquered regions. For performances in various cities, Albinoni's setting of *Pimpinone* was not always the selected version. At least two other composers are known to have provided musical settings of the *Pimpinone* libretto: Francesco Conti's setting was performed in Vienna in 1717 and in Brunswick in 1720 and 1731; Georg Telemann's setting (of a revised German-language libretto) was performed in Hamburg in 1725 and 1730.

Before the advent of the comic intermezzo, Italian opera had not possessed repertory works in the modern sense (i.e., works that are regularly revived in basically unaltered form). The performing material of seventeenth- and eighteenth-century operas remained in the custody of composers and impresarios, who did not scruple to adapt the music to the vocal ranges and capabilities of the particular singers engaged (and to the taste of particular audiences), and who often altered the original work almost beyond recognition. However, because roles in the comic intermezzi were predetermined according to sex and vocal range, the singers in these productions probably traveled from performance to performance with their own copies of the music. Certainly, arias might be added, subtracted, or exchanged for others, but the narrow margin for improvement in the recitatives ensured that, except in the fairly unusual event of a complete new setting of an intermezzo libretto by another composer, the main body of the work remained in its original form. (The fact that the libretto of *Pimpinone* was set by no less than three composers—Albinoni, Conti, and Telemann—can be explained by reference to special factors.)[21]

Naples remained surprisingly resistant to comic intermezzi on the Venetian pattern until the 1720s, preferring to retain the *scene buffe* loosely associated with the opera (see above). Gordana Lazarevich observes that the 1709 production of *Pimpinone* in its original form in Naples was "an unusual occurrence for a city in which foreign intermezzi were, as a rule, slightly altered, with at least the substitution of one aria or duet by a domestic composer."[22] Even here, however, the influence of the typically Neapolitan *scene buffe* can be seen in the manner in which the score relating to the Naples performance is laid out: Intermezzo I is positioned and described as Scene 15 of Act I of the opera *Engelberta* (in a setting by Orefici and Mancini); Intermezzo II is identified as Scene 20 of Act II; and Intermezzo III appears without a scene number after Scene 6 of Act III.[23] In the corresponding libretto for this Naples 1709 production, the intermezzi are grouped together after the opera; but the fact that the libretti of opera and intermezzi are published in a single volume with continuous pagination is evidence of an attempt to assimilate the new-style intermezzi to the practice of comic scenes.

In the early 1720s an important school of Neapolitan opera composers (e.g., Vinci, Porpora, and Leo) became dominant in Venice and in its traditional area of operatic influence (centers such as Vicenza, Verona, and Rovigo). Some Neapolitan composers settled for long periods in Venice. Through this activity they became acquainted with, and began to cultivate, the intermezzo in its final (Venetian) form, which they also took to Naples itself. Pergolesi's famous *La serva padrona* (1733) is a representative work of this phase of intermezzo composition.

In many centers the comic intermezzo was no longer performed by the middle of the century; public taste swung toward ballets, and the comic element became reabsorbed by the conventional opera.[24]

Ironically, the literary status of the comic intermezzo was given an early boost by the Venetian censors. Noting that the libretti of intermezzi were normally left in manuscript state, which enabled singers to make unlicensed alterations to the previously approved text with little risk of detection, the censors decreed on 1 October 1707 that in the future, intermezzi libretti would be published in the same manner as opera libretti.[25] Publication of the libretti aided both the spread and the recognition of the new genre, and the comic intermezzo soon aroused the interest of literary connoisseurs and bibliophiles. Perhaps because they feared the scorn of more serious-minded colleagues, the intermezzo librettists were at first generally unwilling to identify themselves. In 1723 an unknown Milanese publisher, using the pseudonym Ipigeo Lucas and giving Amsterdam as the place of publication, brought out a two-volume anthology entitled *Raccolta copiosa d'intermedj*.[26] This collection contained texts for fifty-four sets of intermezzi, including *Pimpinone*.[27] It is noteworthy that in the second, "Neapolitan" phase of intermezzo composition, the authorship of libretti becomes more frequently acknowledged—evidence, possibly, of increasing acceptance of this genre.

Pimpinone: The Libretto

It would be only a slight exaggeration to say that the libretto of *Pimpinone* exists in as many versions as there are editions. The twenty-two extant libretti bear out Troy's happily expressed observation that "the degree of similarity between two versions of the same libretto tends to diminish as their separation in time and place of publication increases."[28] (See the Appendix on p. xxvi for identification of the sigla used below and for further information concerning the various libretti and performances.) The relationship among the text sources is complicated by the fact that the earliest published libretto (1708a) presents a version of the text that differs in several details (see Critical Notes) from that of the earliest extant musical source and its associated libretto (1709a).[29] Such discrepancies are common in baroque opera, and one must assume either that Pariati retouched the text at the time it went to press, or that amendments were made to the text as supplied (presumably in manuscript) to Albinoni. (Although this manuscript is now lost, it has been possible to reconstruct its contents, at least in part, by working backwards from the various extant text forms.) Interestingly, there are also significant textual differences between the text underlaid in the score and that in the libretto of the 1709 Naples production, and this discrepancy suggests that some final modifications were introduced by the composer himself. Most of the libretti used in subsequent performances (particularly those that can be identified with the central tradition of performance represented by Cavana and, later, Ungarelli) cumulatively modify the putative lost manuscript version; exceptions are the libretti for the Milan

(1709b) and Vicenza (1712a) productions, which reprint the 1708a version of the libretto without significant alteration.[30] In view of Pariati's presence in Vienna at the time, it is not surprising that Conti's setting (1717a) also reverts to the "official," polished 1708 version;[31] this time the libretto corresponds to the text underlaid in the score.

Many libretti are based to a greater or lesser extent on earlier libretti that were updated to take account of new arias. Thus, the libretto of the later Parma production (1724a) is related to that of the earlier production (1714a); the two Bologna libretti (1717b and 1728a) are similarly related. In regard to spelling and punctuation, printers and editors followed their own inclinations. Thus, the libretto of the Florence production (1718a) consistently restores final E's (e.g., "servire" for "servir") when prosody permits.

The poetic style and versification of *Pimpinone* retain most of the formulae of *opera seria*. Recitative verse is written in *versi sciolti* (generally unrhymed lines of either seven or eleven syllables). Aria verse is cast in the familiar two-stanza form, with the first stanza repeated in *da capo* fashion. However, the aria texts in this set of intermezzi contain a greater number of lines than one would expect in an *opera seria* aria written in the same meter; this is, as Troy points out,[32] because of the relative absence of coloratura and the preference for a rapid, declamatory style of delivery. Another typical intermezzo trait is the fondness for stichomythia in duets: the characters take alternate lines, or—when the lines are sufficiently long—they take alternate hemistiches. Recitative lines, too, become fragmented more often than in *opera seria*, and this imparts a realistic cut and thrust to the dialogue.

The theme and plot of *Pimpinone* have been examined by several writers.[33] Vespetta ("little wasp") and Pimpinone are the stock eighteenth-century intermezzo characters of a *servetta* (servant) and a *vecchio* (old man); their more realistic character types embody the change in *dramatis personae* from the *paggio* and *vecchia* (old woman) of the seventeenth-century intermezzi. In the first intermezzo of the set, Vespetta succeeds, through flattery and promises of exemplary behavior, in gaining employment with Pimpinone, a rich bachelor. In the second intermezzo, Vespetta, having taken over the reins of Pimpinone's household, threatens to leave because of Pimpinone's spendthrift ways and because of the rumors regarding their relationship. Pimpinone swallows the bait and offers marriage on condition that Vespetta promises (which she does) to act as a frugal *cittadina* and refrain from high living. The third intermezzo begins with a remonstration by Pimpinone, who sees his new wife about to go out for an evening's amusement. Vespetta declares that she has no intention of keeping her prenuptial promises. When Pimpinone talks of beating her with a stick, Vespetta indignantly threatens to divorce him. Realizing his practical and emotional dependence on her and recoiling from the prospect of repaying her dowry (which he himself had put up), Pimpinone reluctantly gives in.

Much of the humor derives from the well-worn antitheses: youth versus age; male versus female; wealth versus impecuniosity; gullibility versus guile. Yet the most interesting antithesis is one that presents Pimpinone as the normal and Vespetta as the deviant character. Pimpinone practices the values of thrift and sobriety adhered to by the traditional *cittadino* stratum of Venetian society. Vespetta, the former *popolana*, aspires to the section of *bourgeoisie* that wishes to emulate the social life of the nobility. In the early eighteenth century, the boundaries between the nobility and the citizenry were breaking down. On one hand, the wealthier citizens were adopting the lifestyle of the nobility and, in some cases, becoming admitted to it; on the other hand, a section of the nobility, the *barnabotti*,[34] was becoming impoverished. The result was a weakening of social norms, summed up by Vespetta's comment "Oggidí l'uso non falla" ("Today everything goes"; see Text and Translation, line 28).

Vespetta's descriptions of the pastimes of the nobility thus satirize not only these pursuits in themselves, but also her wish to engage in them. In lines 37–47 we have a reference to *cicisbeismo*, the courting of married ladies by young gallants. Lines 143–153 poke fun at the coquetry and *décolletage* of society ladies. In his catalogue of vices that Vespetta must avoid (lines 156–161), Pimpinone mentions exhibiting oneself on a balcony, banqueting, theater-going, dancing, gambling, attending parties, reading books about love, and going about masked. Vespetta adds to the list speaking French, dressing up, and playing the popular card game *manilla* (lines 235–242).[35]

Pariati's attitude concerning these activities is ambiguous. (He was himself no model of correct social behavior!) We must be careful not to project backwards in time our view of the later *opera buffa* as an artform that represents emergent middle-class values. The audiences who attended performances of *Pimpinone* retained, by and large, the world-view of the aristocracy, on whose subsidies the very existence of opera still depended. Nevertheless, Pariati leaves us free either to sympathize with Vespetta, but scorn her aspirations, or to sympathize with the aspirations, but scorn her *parvenu* behavior.

Pimpinone: The Music

None of the three surviving sources of the music for the setting of *Pimpinone* in the present edition names Albinoni as the composer, and none gives a formal title to the work. All three are manuscripts. In the first, the three intermezzi appear ostensibly as *scene buffe* in an archival score of the opera *Engelberta* (Naples, 1709), a joint composition of Antonio Orefici and Francesco Mancini.[36] This manuscript, the only complete source for *Pimpinone*, is now held by the Österreichische Nationalbibliothek; it will be referred to below as Source A. The second source of music for this setting of *Pimpinone* is found as the last part of an archival score of Caldara's pastorale *La costanza in amor vince l'inganno* (Rome, 1711), of which only the first volume, containing Act I and Intermezzo I, has been preserved.[37] This manuscript is now held by the Diözesan-Bibliothek, Münster; it will be referred to below as Source B. Ursula Kirkendale has identified the copyist of this manuscript as Tarquinio Lanciani, whose invoice concerning the work was receipted on 28 February 1711 by his collaborator and probable relative Francesco Antonio Lanciani.[38] The third source consists only of vocal and instrumental parts for Vespetta's aria "Chi mi vuol?" (No. 1). It comes from an anthology of Italian operatic arias preserved in Schwerin,[39] and will be referred to below as Source C. The collection includes eight other arias individually attributed to Albinoni, of which one ("Stelle ingrate") is of identified provenance.[40] Each piece within its respective partbook in the anthology is headed "dell'opera Sign. Albinoni." If the convincing stylistic evidence supporting Albinoni (see below) is not considered, this heading might mean only that the aria "Chi mi vuol?" occurred during an opera by Albinoni, for which the intermezzi could have been written by another composer. The only known productions of *Pimpinone* in which both opera and intermezzi are by Albinoni are those listed in the Appendix as 1708a and 1722a. However, the Schwerin aria cannot relate to the 1722a production, in which the present "Chi mi vuol?" was replaced by a new aria. Nor is it likely to relate to the 1708a production, since one interesting feature of the Schwerin source is the dotting of many of the groups of equal sixteenths also found in the other two sources for the music of *Pimpinone*. (The dotting makes explicit a form of rhythmic assimilation that probably always occurred in the performance of this aria, following the performance practice of the time.) Thus, the Schwerin source is likely to be later than the other two extant musical sources. There remains the possibility that the copyist of the Schwerin anthology used the term "opera" laxly, out of ignorance or habit, but this cannot be proved.

Style analysis must therefore guide us to the identity of the composer. Fortunately, Albinoni's musical language is so full of idiosyncrasy, that evidence to prove his authorship is not hard to assemble. We find the familiar square-cut rhythms and short, breathless instrumental phrases (No. 9, mm. 1–3); the sudden introduction of new counterpoints in a playful spirit (No. 1, mm. 25–27, and No. 3, mm. 19–21); the criss-crossing lines that paraphrase rather than imitate one another (No. 5, mm. 1–4); the bass parts in a high register that are given to upper strings and that often rise above the "middle" parts to create unorthodox second-inversion chords (No. 9, *passim*); the fondness for passing $^6_3$ or $^8_3$ chords on the supertonic (No. 1, m. 12 and No. 9, m. 1); the peculiar form of plagal cadence that arises from the substitution of a $^6_3$ for a $^5_3$ chord on the subdominant (No. 5, m. 2); and the cultivation of complex part-writing in several independent contrapuntal voices (No. 9, mm. 18–22). A comparison of the music with that of Albinoni's contribution to an exactly contemporary setting of *Engelberta* (i.e., the Venice, 1709 setting—not the setting for Naples by Orefici and Mancini referred to above) strengthens the argument that Albinoni is the composer of the intermezzi.[41]

Circumstantial evidence is also in Albinoni's favor. Troy states tentatively that intermezzi were written, as a rule, by the composer of the opera with which they were originally performed.[42] This is an assumption, explicit or tacit, that most modern writers have made, and one that seems reasonable at the level of a generalization, albeit more on commonsense grounds than through the weight of evidence. If one uses this theory to identify intermezzo composers, one must first be certain, of course, that both the opera in question and the accompanying intermezzi were receiving their first performance. This was indeed the case with the 1708 production in Venice of *Astarto* and *Pimpinone* (1708a). On that basis, Albinoni is the likely composer of the original *Pimpinone*. One must observe, however, that several writers have made the mistake of assuming that subsequent productions of *Pimpinone* with other operas necessarily employed new settings of Pariati's libretto by the composers of those operas. Thus, Mamczarz and the Kirkendales identify the composer of the 1711 score for Rome as Caldara;[43] Mamczarz attributes the composition of the 1725 score for Venice to Marc'Antonio Ziani (to whom she also mistakenly attributes the opera), and that of the 1728 score for Bologna to Buini.[44] Less explicably, Lazarevich names Gasparini as the composer of the original (1708) setting,[45] while Cvetko (speaking of the 1740 production) cites Buini again.[46]

If we accept the theory that Albinoni was the composer of the 1708 setting of *Pimpinone*, we can be fairly sure, for reasons given earlier (see p. ix), that, except in the case of added or substituted numbers, his music continued to be used in all performances belonging to the central tradition. We should be more cautious about the versions performed from 1725 onward. For example, a puzzling feature of the 1725a libretto is that it closely follows the text of the 1711b libretto, reverting to the "Chi mi vuol?" opening aria (absent since 1716), but yet it includes the additional aria "Ella mi vuol confondere" (not found before 1715). This rather eclectic form of text hints at the possibility that the libretto was assembled in preparation for a new setting by another composer. But perhaps a vital link—a libretto dating from ca. 1715 and containing both "Chi mi vuol?" and "Ella mi vuol confondere"—has been lost, in which case the 1725a libretto might still be connected with the central tradition.

Albinoni's setting of *Pimpinone* is typical of the early comic intermezzo as composed by Gasparini and Lotti. The orchestra is confined to four-part strings with continuo, and the orchestral role is more restricted than in opera proper. Two arias in *Pimpinone* (Nos. 7 and 11) are accompanied by continuo alone; the final duet (No. 15) requires the orchestra solely for a ritornello rounding off the "A" section. Elsewhere, the instruments are often silent in the sections with voice, and their ritornelli are notably concise. This desire for brevity is illustrated by the fact that the *Devise* (Hugo Riemann's term for a "motto" phrase first sung on its own and then repeated after an instrumental interjection to introduce the first vocal section) is entirely absent in *Pimpinone*, notwithstanding its great popularity in opera arias of the time (including those of Albinoni's *Engelberta*). The duets, unlike those in opera, eschew lyricism in favor of a quasi-conversational exchange of staccato phrases. Albinoni's liking for a style of counterpoint that emphasizes the distinctiveness rather than the similarity of two lines adds to the realism. All things considered, however, the musical language of Albinoni's intermezzi resembles that of his operas to a greater degree than one finds when making the same comparison for Scarlatti, Orlandini, or Vinci. This is partly a Venetian characteristic, and partly a consequence of Albinoni's stylistic inflexibility. It is a pity that the music of two later sets of intermezzi by him, *Malsazio e Fiammetta* (Rome, 1726) and *Il Satrapone* (Pavia, 1729, and Prague, 1729) is lost, for it might show the same progress towards the *galant* that we see in the surviving arias of his operas *L'incostanza schernita* (1727) and *Ardelinda* (1732).

No assessment of Albinoni's *Pimpinone* can avoid a comparison with Telemann's 1725 setting of a version of the same text. Since its appearance in a modern edition by Theodor W. Werner in 1936,[47] the Telemann *Pimpinone* has become one of the most frequently performed baroque stage works. Telemann's work is a masterpiece that outclasses Albinoni's setting in musical invention and depth of characterization. Albinoni's timid forays into the tenor register to portray two gossiping women in Pimpinone's aria "So quel che si dice" (No. 11) pale into insignificance beside Telemann's outrageously comic alternation of the soprano and alto registers, sung in a falsetto voice. Telemann's final number, a bittersweet duet in the style of a Polish dance, achieves a far more interesting dramatic resolution than Albinoni's frantic but rather colorless duet of insults.

The virtues of Albinoni's *Pimpinone* are more modest than those of Telemann's. One notes a sure sense of style, a firm control of proportion, and an original feeling for melody—qualities that Conti's somewhat more ambitious setting of this same text lacks.[48] Albinoni's *Pimpinone* offers a good specimen of the intermezzo genre in its initial phase; it is also an excellent introduction to his operatic music.

The Edition

The music of the present edition is based on the manuscript score contained in the music of *Engelberta* (see p. xi), Source A. The Münster score (Source B) and Schwerin parts (Source C) have been collated in the relevant numbers. The text underlaid in the edition follows that of Source A. However, five other text sources (the underlaid texts in sources B and C and three early libretti) were also consulted, and these sources have been used to supply emendations where necessary to correct errors in the literary text of this principal source (see Critical Notes).

Square brackets distinguish editorial additions in the form of names of instruments and characters, description and numbering of individual movements, tempo directions, time signatures, notes, ties, rests, trills, fermatas, explanatory rhythmic signs, and underlaid text (including repetitions indicated by the sign ✌ in the source). Slurs that link notes sung to the same syllable are added tacitly, however. Editorial chromatic inflection is shown by enclosing the accidental concerned in square brackets, unless the note is governed (in modern notation) by an accidental occurring earlier in the same measure; in such cases the omission of the accidental in the source is cited in the Critical Notes. Cautionary accidentals of editorial origin are enclosed in parentheses. Rhythmic signs placed over the staff suggest a manner of performance consistent with baroque principles of rhythmic assimilation. The upper staff of the continuo part contains an editorial realization of the generally unfigured bass. The accompaniment of the recitatives is presented in a deliberately skeletal form; performers are advised to thicken the chords with extra harmony notes, and, perhaps, *acciaccature* (dissonant notes struck with the chord and quickly released). Francesco Gasparini's *L'armonico pratico al cembalo* (Venice, 1708) furnishes many useful hints.[49]

Note heads in parentheses indicate the pitch of the appoggiaturas that would by convention have been sung in the recitatives to replace the penultimate note of a phrase. This has been done because in recent years musicologists have reached a consensus on the desirability of "foreshortening" cadences—performing them in the notated rhythm, so that the end of the vocal phrase (typically, the keynote preceded by an appoggiatura) coincides with the dominant chord in the accompaniment.[50]

The spelling and punctuation of the text have been normalized to conform to modern Italian usage, al-

though archaic forms (e.g., "deggio" for "devo") have been retained. The part of Vespetta, notated in the alto clef in the original sources, now appears in the treble clef.

Problems of performance are few. It is unclear whether the *Adagio* marking, expressive of mock sentimentality, in measure 31 of No. 9 should remain in force for the rest of the "B" section. If not, it would be appropriate to revert to *Allegro* at the end of measure 32.

Critical Notes

The Text

This section is in two parts. The first part (Variant Readings) lists discrepancies between the text underlaid in the edition and that of the six sources deemed of greatest relevance to the present edition. These text sources are: the underlaid text in the score relating to the 1709 Naples production, Vienna, Österreichische Nationalbibliothek, Ms. 18057 (Source A); the corresponding libretto (1709a); the underlaid text in the score of Intermezzo I relating to the 1711 Rome production with Caldara's *La costanza in amor vince l'inganno* (Source B); the corresponding libretto (1711a); the underlaid text in the parts for the opening aria, "Chi mi vuol?," preserved in Schwerin (Source C); the libretto of the 1708 Venice production (1708a). Typographical errors have been corrected tacitly, and the spelling and punctuation of the variant readings have been regularized in the manner described above under The Edition. Each text citation is preceded by the appropriate line number to locate it within the libretto as a whole.

The second part of this section (Textual Revisions) records the addition, substitution or omission of arias and duets in different productions of *Pimpinone*, as ascertained from extant libretti. Productions are identified by their year and letter (See Appendix). No account has been taken of amendments to the original arias and duets. Abbreviations in this section are as follows: L = line; V. = Vespetta; and P. = Pimpinone.

VARIANT READINGS

L. 6, E mi aggiusto al mal, al bene (C); E mi aggiusto al male e al bene (1708a, 1709a); E m'aggiusto al male e al bene (1711a). L. 12, Che buon padron saria per me. Vediamo. (1708a, 1709a). L. 18, (Se costui mi accettasse . . .) (1708a). L. 20, (Seco pur volontier mi aggiusterei.) (1708a). L. 23, Ch'io non L'avea veduta in verità. (A, B, 1709a, 1711a). L. 26, Ch'insegna ov'io servia io l'ho imparate. (A). L. 27, Gran dama la padrona esser doveva. (1709a). L. 29, Adesso il "mi la sol," il "la la la la" (1708a); Adesso il "mi la sol,"/ Il "la la la ra la" (1711a). L. 38, Or que' fiori, or quei fogli, or quei ritratti, (A); Or quei fiori, or quei fogli, or que' ritratti, (B); Or que' fiori, or que' fogli, or que' ritratti,

xiii

(1708a, 1711a). L. 39, Un mondo di ambasciate e di risposte. (1708a). L. 40, Non mi faccia piú dir. Io son segreta. (1708a); Non mi facci più dir ch'io son segreta. (1711a). L. 43, Discolpa ognì difetto, e vuol che sia. (1708a). L. 45, Ma quanti ha geni poi la signorina? (A). L. 47, Deggio dirne anche il ben: non ha che sei. (A, B). L. 51, Come a dir sul mattin pria di acconciarsi, (1708a). L. 61, Verbi grazia . . . il vorrei . . . (1708a). L. 62, (Quanto val esser bello!) Ebben, che dici? (1708a). L. 78, Un patron piú dabben non vidi mai. L. 83, Lascia adesso i complimenti. (1708a). L. 84, Si contenti, si contenti. (1708a). L. 86, Illustrissimo patron! (A, B); Io mi umilio al mio padron (1708a); (È pur pazzo il mio padron.) (1711a). Ll. 86–87, O felice Pimpinon. (1708a; this line, which, as l. 95, closes the "B" section of the duet, is erroneously appended to the "A" section.) L. 89, Su la man. Qui niun c'osserva. (A, B, 1709a). L. 90, Troppo onore. Io son Sua serva. (1708a). L. 102, E sa il Ciel se mi duol fin nell'interno. (1708a, 1711a). L. 105, No, sinché avrete (1708a, 1711a). L. 106, Quella chiave alla man, no, no'l farete. (1708a). L. 114, Oggi me la comprai con venti scudi. (1709a). L. 117, E con essa comprai questi orecchini. (1708a, 1711a). L. 121, Guarda un poco in questi occhi di foco, (1708a). L. 135, Per far tacer ognun v'è il suo rimedio. (1708a, 1711a). L. 136, Per chi nacque a servir io non lo veggio. (1711a). L. 152, Per mostrar a' piú golosi (1708a); Per mostrar ai piú gelosi (1711a). L. 160, Maschera . . . Non so dir com'ella sia. (A, 1709a, 1711a). L. 162, Son sua serva in ogni stato. (A). L. 173, V. (Me ne rido.) P. (Non v'è prezzo.) (1709a). L. 176, V., (Non v'è alcuno.) P., (Non l'ha alcuna.) (1711a). L. 178, This line is given to both characters in Albinoni's setting. L. 179, V., Parlo, o caro. (A); V., Parto, o caro. (1711a; Pimpinone's hemistich is omitted). L. 181, Line absent in 1708a and 1711a. L. 183, (Oh, questa è brutta!) Io 'l vo' sapere adesso.(A). L. 186, A spasso? E questo è il patto? (1711a). L. 192, (O che flemma mi vuol! Che feci mai?) (1708a). L. 197, Illustrissima, sí. (Sono in malora.) (1708a). L. 202, Vado a passar il dí con mia comare. (1708a). L. 206, "Strissima, Strissima, come si sta?" (1708a); "Sustrissima, come si sta?" (1709a); "Lustrissima, come si sta?" (1711a). L. 208, È pur stravagante, è pure indiscreto. (1708a). L. 210, E l'altra risponde: "Gran bestia ch'egli è." (1708a). L. 214, S'ei dice, "no no," io dico, "sí sí." (1708a). L. 217, Del "presto" non m'impegno. Infino sera. (1709a). L. 222, Maledico il dolor che ho in questo dente. (1708a). L. 245, Non si può! Quella roba è mia. (A; this reading is retained in the present underlaid text—the "Quella roba è roba mia" given in the Text and Translation section appears there to ensure proper poetic scansion.) L. 249, E s'io facessi un dí che con la moglie. (1708a). L. 261, Sí, Vespettina mia, fa quel che vuoi. (1708a). L. 263, Quel che so far, bell'uomini, vedrete. (1709a). L. 277, V., Parla su! P., Mi duol il dente. (1711a).

TEXTUAL REVISIONS

L. 1, substituted aria (V.) "Eh non giova l'esser buona" (1716a, 1717b, 1718a, 1723a, 1724a); substituted aria (V.) "Alle volte io non vorrei" (1722a). After l. 30, additional aria (V.) "Höflich reden, lieblich singen" (1725b, 1730a). After l. 58, additional aria (P.) "Ella mi vuol confondere" (1715a, 1716a, 1717b, 1718a, 1722a, 1723a, 1725a, 1725b, 1725c, 1728a, 1730a, 1740a). After l. 66, addtional aria (P.) "La favorita / Di Pimpinon" (1709b). After l. 100, additional aria (V.) "Nei brievi momenti" (1725a, 1725b, 1730a, 1740a). L. 205, omitted aria (P.) "So quel che si dice, e quel che si fa" (1725c, 1728a); substituted aria (P.) "Gran Diavola! Per collera" (1717a). L. 235, substituted aria (V.) "Nel gran mondo tutto brio" (1722a). After 253, additional duet "Wilde Hummel, böser Engel" (1725b). L. 265, substituted duet "Schweig hinkünftig, albrer Tropf" (1725b). As the lines of J. P. Praetorius's version of the libretto for 1725 b (see entries for ll. 253 and 265) do not correspond, in the latter part of Intermezzo III, to those of the Italian original, the line numbers given here refer to the closest equivalent in the Italian text.

The Music

Note that whereas Source A is complete, Source B contains only the music of the first intermezzo (Nos. 1–3), and Source C has only the first aria of Intermezzo I. (See *Pimpinone: The Music* for a detailed description of the music sources.) When no source is specified in the Critical Notes entries below, the reading cited occurs in all of the sources containing the measure or measures in question.

It is impossible to regard any one source among the three as being the most reliable or authoritative—either empirically or on philological grounds. When a choice of readings has occurred, the editor has preferred whichever reading seemed stylistically or grammatically closest to the norms of Albinoni's music. Indeed, the high degree of correspondence between the musical and literary texts of Sources A and B indicates that the two scores may well have been copied from the same source (perhaps a working copy in Cavana's possession). Abbreviations used in this section are as follows: M. = measure; vn. = violin; vla. = viola. Pitches are given according to the Helmholtz system, wherein c' = middle C, c" = the C above middle C, and so forth.

[1. ARIA]

Source C has the time-signature ₵ in all parts. M. 1, vn. 2, notes 5–8 are sixteenths in Source B. M. 3, vn. 1, notes 5–12 are sixteenths in Sources A and B; vn. 2, notes 3 and 4 are sixteenths in Sources A and B; bass, notes 1 and 2 are sixteenths in Sources A and B, a dotted eighth and a sixteenth in Source C. M. 4, vn. 1, notes 1–8 and 10–13 are sixteenths in Sources A and B; vla., note 7 is a' in Source A; bass, note 2 is g in Source A. M. 5, vn. 1, notes 1–4 are sixteenths in Sources A and B; bass, note 1 is a sixteenth in Source C, and notes 2 and 3 are sixteenths in Sources A and B. M. 7, bass, notes 1 and 2 are sixteenths in Source C. M. 9, vn. 1, notes 2–5 are sixteenths in Sources A and B; vn. 2, notes 2 and 3 are sixteenths in Sources A and B; bass, note 1 is a sixteenth in Source C. M. 10, vn. 1, notes 9 and 10 are sixteenths in Source B; vn. 2, notes 1, 2, 9, 10, 11, and 12 are sixteenths in Sources A and B; vla., note 1 is d′ in Source C. M. 12, vn. 1, note 10 has the sign + (denoting a trill) above it in Source C. M. 13, V., note 3 is a quarter-note, and note 4 is a g′ in Source C. M. 15, vn. 1, notes 2 and 3 are sixteenths in Sources A and B; bass, note 1 is a sixteenth in Source C. M. 16, vn. 1, all notes in this m. are sixteenths in Sources A and B; vn. 2, notes 4 and 5 are sixteenths in Source A. M. 17, vn. 1, note 3 has the sign + (denoting a trill) in Source C; vn. 1 and vn. 2, notes 5 and 6 are sixteenths in Sources A and B; bass, note 1 is rendered as two sixteenths (a and b) in Source C. M. 18, bass, notes 1 and 2 are sixteenths in Sources A and B. M. 19, vn. 1, notes 3–12 are sixteenths in Sources A and B; vn. 2, notes 3 and 4 are sixteenths in Sources A and B; bass, notes 1 and 2 are sixteenths in Sources A and B. M. 20, vn. 1, notes 1–8 and 10–13 are sixteenths in Sources A and B. M. 21, vn. 1, notes 1–4 are sixteenths in Sources A and B; vn. 2, notes 2 and 3 are sixteenths in Sources A and B; vla., notes 2 and 3 are sixteenths in Source C; bass, note 1 is a sixteenth in Source C, and notes 2 and 3 are sixteenths in Sources A and B. M. 22, bass, notes 4 and 5 are sixteenths in Source C. M. 26, vn. 1, Sources A and B omit the tie between notes 5 and 6. M. 27, V., notes 5 and 6 are eighths in Source C; vn. 1, a dotted sixteenth-note (a′′) and a thirty-second-note (g′′) appear after the rest (as a cue for the *da capo* repeat) in Sources A and B, Source C has a quarter-rest in place of the eighth-rest; V. and bass, the rest is a quarter-rest in all sources; vn. 2, vla., all sources have a single whole-rest.

[2. RECITATIVO]
Mm. 1–2, bass, note 1 of m. 1 is a whole-note, and note 2 is omitted, and m. 2 has two half-notes (c♯ and d); since the $\frac{5}{2}$ chord in the second half of m. 1 implied by the reading in Source A is uncharacteristic of Albinoni, the more conventional reading in Source B has been preferred here. Mm. 4–5, bass, Source B omits the tie across the barline. Mm. 8–9, bass, Source B omits the tie across the barline. M. 13, P., note 10 has no flat. Mm. 14–15, bass, Source B omits the tie across the barline. M. 21, bass, note 1, the sharp appears as a bass figure above the d in Source A. M. 27, V., note 7 has no sharp. M. 32, V., note 5 has no sharp. M. 37, V., notes 3 and 5 have no sharp. Mm. 50–51, bass, Source B omits the tie across the barline. M. 52, bass, notes 1 and 2, Source B omits the tie. M. 63, V., cropping has removed the syllable "zar" from the underlaid text in Source A. M. 66, all parts, in place of this measure, Source B has an extension by two beats of m. 65; the bass note (B) is reduced to a half-note, and the quarter-rests on both sides of the barline (i.e., in mm. 65 and

66) in the voice part are omitted—whether this is the original form for this music or a subsequent adaptation for the purpose of speeding up the pace is an open question. M. 72, bass, notes 2–3, Source B omits the tie. M. 73, V., note 4 has a natural sign in Source A. M. 79, V., note 3 has no flat. M. 90, bass, note 1 rendered as two tied half-notes in Source A, and as two half-notes in Source B. M. 117, V., note 5 has no sharp. M. 119, V., the rest is a quarter-rest.

[3. DUETTO]
Source B has the tempo marking *Allegro assai*. M. 15, P., the underlaid text is complete only in Source B. M. 19, V., notes 5 and 7 are a′ in Source B. M. 23, V., note 5 is d′. M. 25, P., the underlaid text is complete only in Source B. M. 47, P., the underlaid text is complete in Source B. M. 52, vn. 1, vn. 2, vla., and V., the measure is occupied by a whole-rest; P. and bass, an eighth-rest follows the quarter-rest.

[4. RECITATIVO]
M. 12, P., note 5 has no flat. M. 29, P., note 5 has no flat.

[5. ARIA]
M. 6, bass, note 6 is A. M. 8, bass, note 3 has no sharp. M. 20, bass, the figure 6 is above note 5. M. 27, vn. 1, vn. 2, and vla. have a quarter-rest.

[7. ARIA]
M. 25, V., note 6 has no natural; bass, note 1 is e. M. 26, V., note 6 has no natural.

[8. RECITATIVO]
M. 15, V., note 3 of this m. is g′. M. 26, P., notes 5–7 of this m. are b, c′, d′.

[9. DUETTO]
M. 3, vn. 1, note 1 is a sixteenth. M. 5, vn. 1, note 3 is f′′, and notes 5 and 6 are e′′ and f′′. M. 12, P., note 1 is b. M. 23, vn. 2, note 1 is f′′. M. 26, bass, note 3 is g. M. 30, V., note 7 has no sharp. M. 33, P., note 6 is c′; bass, note 1 is c. M. 37, P., notes 1 and 4 are both c′.

[10. RECITATIVO]
M. 5, V., note 5 has no flat. M. 18, V., note 4 has a natural.

[11. ARIA]
P. and bass, the key–signature has F–sharp and C–sharp only.

[12. RECITATIVO]
M. 1, P., note 5 has no sharp. M. 11, P., note 3 has no flat. M. 27, P., note 4 has no flat.

[13. ARIA]
M. 24, vn. 1, vn. 2, vla., and V., note 1 is a half–note.

[14. RECITATIVO]
M. 21, V., note 7 has no sharp. M. 22, V., note 5 has no sharp. M. 23, P., note 3 has no sharp.

Acknowledgments

The editor and publisher would like to thank the authorities of the Österreichische Nationalbibliothek, Vienna; the Diözesan-Bibliothek, Münster; and the Mecklenburgische Landesbibliothek, Schwerin, for their permission to use source material in their possession for the preparation of this edition. Moreover, the preparation of this edition has been greatly facilitated by the kind help of many scholars, among whom the editor would like to name David Bryant, Bojan Bujić, Pierluigi Petrobelli, Paul Raspé, Claudio Sartori, Eleanor Selfridge-Field, and Reinhard Strohm. The editor is also grateful to the University of Liverpool for financial assistance.

Michael Talbot
June 1982
Liverpool

Notes

1. The most extensive accounts of Albinoni's life and music are those given in Remo Giazotto, *Tomaso Albinoni* (Milan, 1945) and in Michael Talbot, *Albinoni. Leben und Werk* (Adliswil, 1980).

2. Francesco Caffi, manuscript notes (ca. 1850) for *Storia della musica teatrale in Venezia* (Venice, Biblioteca Nazionale Marciana, Cod. It. IV–747 [= 10462–10465], 10465), fol. 39^r.

3. Venice, Archivio I.R.E. (= Istituzioni di Ricovero e di Educazione), Der. 56, G. 2, n. 48, fascicolo "musica," inserto 47. I am grateful to Don Gastone Vio for bringing this document to my attention.

4. Until the extinction of the Republic in 1797, the Venetians used a calendar in which the months of January and February belonged to the outgoing instead of the incoming year. Thus, any day in January or February 1750, *more veneto* (Venetian style), is equivalent to the same day in 1751, modern style.

5. The remainder of Albinoni's instrumental music consists of: (1) three collections of sonatas (totaling seventeen works) and a solitary concerto, all published without opus number; and (2) four concertos and twenty-eight sonatas and *balletti* preserved only in manuscript.

6. Several works may be presumed lost without trace; interestingly, the libretto of Albinoni's penultimate known opera, *Candalide* (1734), speaks of this being his eightieth such work. "Intermezzi" or "set of intermezzi" is used in this Preface to describe the single dramatic entity that consists of two, three, or more intermezzi. Many modern writers employ the singular form "intermezzo" to denote this entity; however, this practice is unfortunate, since it is both illogical (what is inserted "in the middle" is not the work in its entirety, but each of its component parts separately) and at variance with the common usage of the eighteenth century.

7. Caffi, *Storia della musica teatrale in Venezia*, 10465, fol. 39^r.

8. The best source of information on Pariati's life is still Naborre Campanini, *Un precursore del Metastasio* (Florence, 1904). A more complete list of Pariati's works than that provided by Campanini can be found in *Enciclopedia dello spettacolo* (Rome, 1960), VII: cols. 1617–1618.

9. Apostolo Zeno, *Poesie drammatiche* (Venice, 1744), vol. IX.

10. See Ursula Kirkendale, *Antonio Caldara. Sein Leben und seine venezianisch-römischen Oratorien* (Graz-Cologne, 1966), pp. 41–42.

11. It is interesting to note, however, that the published Viennese libretti cite Pariati alone as the author of *Il Costantino* and *Sesostri*, and Zeno alone as the author of *Astarto*.

12. I have been unable to find any source giving the month and day of Pariati's death.

13. The libretto of the intermezzi *Polastrella e Parpagnacco*, first performed in the carnival season of 1708 at the S. Cassiano theater, Venice, is attributed to Pariati in Irène Mamczarz, *Les intermèdes comiques italiens au XVIIIe siècle en France et en Italie* (Paris, 1972), p. 167 and elsewhere, and in Gordana Lazarevich, "The Role of the Neapolitan Intermezzo in the Evolution of Eighteenth-Century Musical Style: Literary, Symphonic and Dramatic Aspects 1685–1735," (Ph. D. diss., Columbia University, 1970), I: 350 and elsewhere. Neither author advances evidence for the attribution. The *Drammaturgia di Lione Allacci accresciuta e continuata fino all'anno MDCCLV* (Venice, 1755), col. 600, describes the libretto as "d'incerto autore."

14. Pariati's *tragicommedie* are: *Anfitrione* (with Zeno, Venice, 1707); *Il finto Policare* (Vienna, 1716); *Don Chisciotte in Sierra Morena* (with Zeno, Vienna, 1719); *Alessandro in Sidone* (with Zeno, Vienna, 1721); *Archelao, re di Cappadozia* (Vienna, 1722); *Creso* (Vienna, 1723); and *Penelope* (Vienna, 1724).

15. Charles E. Troy has produced several scholarly studies on the comic intermezzo. See his "The Comic Intermezzo in Eighteenth-Century *Opera Seria*," (Ph. D. diss., Harvard University, 1972) and his article "Intermezzo (ii)" in *The New Grove Dictionary of Music and Musicians* (1980). Troy's *The Comic Intermezzo: A Study in the History of Eighteenth-Century Italian Opera* (Ann Arbor, 1979) presents the text of his Ph. D. dissertation and promises to become the standard work on the comic intermezzo. Some useful additional information can be found in Mamczarz, *Les intermèdes comiques italiens*, although this study is too careless of detail to be a reliable source of reference on individual works. Lazarevich, "The Role of the Neapolitan Intermezzo," is a valuable adjunct to Troy's wider-ranging study. One should finally mention *Die Musik in Geschichte und Gegenwart*, s.v. "Intermezzo (italienisches Theater)," by Ortrun Landmann and Gordana Lazarevich; this article makes good the failure to cover the genre in the original series of *MGG* volumes.

16. Troy, *The Comic Intermezzo*, pp. 11–14.

17. Lazarevich, "The Role of the Neapolitan Intermezzo,"

p. 33, cites the example of Legrenzi's *Giustino*, first performed in Venice in 1683, which, when taken to Naples in the following year, acquired a set of new comic scenes, for which the words were written by Andrea Perrucci and the music possibly by Alessandro Scarlatti.

18. The intermezzi themselves employed simple scenery that is rarely specified in the libretti. However, the sets described in the libretto of the 1711 Rome production of *Pimpinone* must be typical: Intermezzo I has a "Cortile con colonnate" (courtyard with colonnades), Intermezzo II a "Colonnato" (colonnade), and Intermezzo III a "Cortile con colonne" (courtyard with columns). These directions may indicate that the same set, possibly with minor variations, was to be used for each of the three intermezzi. No other libretto of *Pimpinone* includes a specification of scenery. This Rome 1711 libretto and a few later ones include sparse stage directions that concern the gestures and movements of the characters. All these directions refer to particular productions and did not originate with Pariati.

19. Troy, *The Comic Intermezzo*, pp. 36–37.

20. If the settings of Pariati's libretto by Conti and Telemann are included, Vienna (1717), Brunswick (1720), and Hamburg (1725) can be added to the list of cities in which *Pimpinone* was performed.

21. It is fair to assume that the performance of *Pimpinone* in Vienna stemmed from the presence there of its librettist, Pariati. Since (one assumes) no music was available at that time, a fresh setting—that made by Conti—was required. Another setting (by Telemann) for Hamburg was necessitated by the translation of the recitative texts into German.

22. Lazarevich, "The Role of the Neapolitan Intermezzo," p. 153.

23. Vienna, Österreichische Nationalbibliothek, Ms. 18057, fols. 54ᵛ, 131ʳ, 170ᵛ.

24. The last known Venetian performances of comic intermezzi took place in 1750.

25. Venice, Museo Civico Correr (Biblioteca), MS. P.D. 348, fol. 23, quoted in Olga A. Termini, "Carlo Francesco Pollarolo: his life, time, and music, with emphasis on the operas," (Ph. D. diss., University of Southern California, 1970), p. 186.

26. Italian publishers often substituted the name of a foreign city such as Amsterdam for that of their own in order to evade the scrutiny of the local censorship.

27. *Raccolta copiosa d'intermedj*, vol. I: 410–421. The libretto from which the *Raccolta copiosa* text was derived is not known, but a comparison of variant readings shows that the text was based on a later version, which included the additional aria "Ella mi vuol confondere," of the text found in the libretto of the 1714 Parma production.

28. Troy, *The Comic Intermezzo*, p. 141.

29. The lowercase letters following the citation of a year (e.g., 1708a) identify the libretto in the list presented in the section *Pimpinone: The Productions* (See Appendix, p. xxvi).

30. The Milanese edition contains the additional aria "La favorita/Di Pimpinon."

31. The name "Grilletta" is substituted everywhere for "Vespetta." One aria, "So quel che si dice," is omitted and replaced by "Gran Diavola! Per collera."

32. Troy, *The Comic Intermezzo*, p. 76.

33. See, for example, Andrea Della Corte, *L'opera comica italiana del '700* (Bari, 1923), I: 40–41; Hellmuth Christian Wolff, *Die Barockoper in Hamburg* (Wolfenbüttel, 1957), I: 117–118; and Stanko Škerlj, *Italijansko gledališče v Ljubljani v preteklih stoletjih* (Ljubljana, 1973), pp. 195–197.

34. So called because they commonly lived in the run-down parish of S. Barnaba.

35. Wolff's description in *Die Barockoper in Hamburg*, p. 118, of the *manilla* and *spadilla* as "spanische Modetänze" (fashionable dances from Spain) is wide of the mark. The *manilla* is the ten in the card game of the same name, the *spadilla* the ace of spades.

36. Vienna, Österreichische Nationalbibliothek, Ms. 18057. In this source the intermezzi end, respectively, on fols. 67ʳ, 145ᵛ, and 181ʳ.

37. Münster, Diözesan-Bibliothek, Hs. 798a.

38. Kirkendale, *Antonio Caldara*, pp. 58, 105–106, and 365. Inadvertently, the reference on p. 58 suggests that Francesco rather than Tarquinio was the copyist of *Pimpinone*. The score was copied for their employer, Francesco Maria Ruspoli, Prince of Cerveteri.

39. Mecklenburgische Landesbibliothek, 4721 (20).

40. *Astarto* (Act I, Scene 9).

41. Scores in West Berlin, Staatsbibliothek, and Vienna, Österreichische Nationalbibliothek. Albinoni composed the first three acts of the opera, while Gasparini composed the remaining two. Other Albinoni operas surviving complete are *Zenobia, regina de' Palmireni* (Venice, 1694) and *La Statira* (Rome, 1726); two serenatas are also extant.

42. Troy, *The Comic Intermezzo*, p. 41. The same generalization is made in Caffi, *Storia della musica teatrale in Venezia*, 10462, fol. 261ᵛ.

43. Mamczarz, *Les intermèdes comiques italiens*, pp. 205 and 509; Ursula and Warren Kirkendale, "Caldara, Antonio," "Dizionario biografico degli italiani" (Rome, 1973), XVI: 563.

44. Mamczarz, *Les intermèdes comiques italiens*, pp. 195, 290, 454, and 517. The citation of Ziani (ca. 1653–1715) is doubly mistaken, for it was Buini who set *Li sdegni cangiati in amore*; Ziani set an earlier version of Silvani's libretto entitled *Il duello d'amore e di vendetta* (Venice, 1700).

45. Lazarevich, "The Role of the Neapolitan Intermezzo," pp. 153, 349n, 350, and 376.

46. Dragotin Cvetko, *Musikgeschichte der Südslawen*, (Kassel-Ljubljana, 1975), p. 86.

47. Telemann, *Pimpinone*, ed. Theodor W. Werner, Das Erbe deutscher Musik, "Oper und Sologesang" (Mainz, 1936).

48. Contemporary manuscript scores in Vienna, Österreichische Nationalbibliothek, Ms. 17120, and Vienna, Gesellschaft der Musikfreunde in Wien, Q 1205.

49. Available in English as *The Practical Harmonist at the Harpsichord*, trans. Frank S. Stillings, ed. David L. Burrows (New Haven, 1963).

50. See Winton Dean, "The Performance of Recitative in Late Baroque Opera," *Music and Letters* LVIII (1977): 389–402.

Text and Translation

In the text presented below, text-lines are numbered in order to make the Critical Notes citations easier to use. The translation has been made by the editor.

Intermezzo I

Vespetta e Pimpinone

[1. Aria]

    V: Chi mi vuol? Son cameriera.
    Fo di tutto. Pian m'intendo
    Di quel tutto che conviene.
    Son dabbene, son sincera;
5. Non ambisco, non pretendo;
    E m'aggiusto al mal e al bene.
      Chi, etc.

[2. Recitativo]

    V: Cerco la mia ventura,
    Ma per le vie onorate. Un po' di dote
    Farmi vorrei col mio sudor. Ma viene
10. Il signor Pimpinone.
    Nobil non è, ma ricco a canna e sciocco.
    Che buon padron saria per me. Vediam.

    P: Guai a chi è ricco, guai. Per ogni parte
    Ognun mi vuol rubar. Piú tanta gente
15. Non voglio in casa mia. Sia benedetto
    L'uso delle servette. Una di queste
    Per me saria un tesoro . . . Uh! Qui
      Vespetta.

    V: (Se costui m'accettasse . . .)
    P: (Se volesse costei . . .)
20. *V:*⎫
    P:⎭ (Seco pur volentier m'aggiusterei.)

    P: Vespettina gentil, come si sta?
    V: Vossignoria illustrissima perdoni.
    Io non L'avea veduta in verità.
    P: Che belle riverenze!
25. *V:* Dal maestro di ballo
    Ch'insegna ov'io serviva io l'ho imparate.

    P: Gran dama la padrona esser dovea.
    V: Che gran dama? Oggidí l'uso non falla.
    Adesso il "mi la sol," il "la la ra ra"

Vespetta and Pimpinone

[1. Aria]

    V: Who'll have me? I'm a maidservant.
    I can do everything. Without fuss I go
      about
    Any task that needs doing.
    I'm respectable, I'm honest;
5. I've no ambitions, no pretensions;
    And I take the rough with the smooth.
      Who'll have me, etc.

[2. Recitative]

    V: I'm seeking my fortune,
    But by honest means. I'd like to earn
      myself a small dowry
    By my sweat. But here comes
10. Signor Pimpinone.
    He's no nobleman, but he's rolling in
      money and foolish.
    What a good master he'd make for me.
      We'll see.
    P: Woe unto the rich, woe. Wherever I go,
    People all try to rob me. I'll stop having so
      many people
15. In my house. Thank God
    For the custom of keeping maidservants.
      One of those
    Would be a blessing to me . . . Ooh!
      Here's Vespetta.
    V: (If that fellow found me suitable . . .)
    P: (If that lass were willing . . .)
20. *V:*⎫
    P:⎭(I could come to an arrangement with him/
      her.)

    P: Vespetta, my dear, how are you?
    V: May your Lordship forgive me.
    Really, I didn't see you.
    P: What a lovely curtsy!
25. *V:* I learned it from the dancing master
    Who teaches at the place where I was in
      service.
    P: Your mistress must have been a fine lady.
    V: A fine lady, you say? Today everything goes.
    Nowadays, "mi la sol" and "la la ra ra"

30. Troppo è comune. Ognuna canta e balla.

P: A che giova, a che serve un tal diletto?

V: Se non altro, a portare avanti il petto.
P: Bene. Or tu piú non servi?
V: La mia licenza ho chiesta, e l'ho ottenuta.
35. P: (Buona nuova per me.) Per qual cagione?
V: Oh! Non voglio dir mal delle padrone.
P: Ma pur? V: La mia volea ch'io ricevessi
Or quei fiori, or quei fogli, or quei ritratti,
Un mondo d'ambasciate e di risposte.
40. Non mi facci piú dir. Io son segreta.

P: Intendo. Amori, è vero?
V: Non vo' parlar. Credo di sí. Ma l'uso
Discolpa un tal difetto, e vuol che sia
L'amor genio innocente e bizzarria.
45. P: Ma quanti geni ha poi la signorina?

V: Se dissi il mal di lei,
Deggio dirne anche il ben: non n'ha che sei.
Ma poco importa ciò. La mia padrona
Di buon occhio talor non mi vedea.

50. P: Che ingrata! Ma perché? V: Perché talvolta,
Come a dir sul mattin pria d'acconciarsi,
Forse di lei piú bella io le parea.

P: Buona cosa è'l servir un uomo, e solo.
Non è cosí? V: Piacesse al Ciel! Pazienza.
55. Io trovato l'avea; ma tanto brutto . . .
P: Brutto com'io? V: Che dice? Al par d'ogn'altro
Sustrissima è una gioia, un giglio, un sole.

P: (O che care parole!)
Or che pensi di far? V: Cercar padrone.

60. P: Lo troverai. Ma dí: come il vorresti?

V: Verbi grazia . . . vorrei . . .
P: (Quanto val l'esser bello!) Ebben, che dici?

V: Il vorrei, come a dir . . . Vossignoria.

P: Or senti, in casa mia son solo e ricco
65. E, senti, liberal. Se pur ti è caro,
Mia cameriera adesso io ti dichiaro.
V: Mi vuol burlar. (La mia fortuna è fatta.)

P: Dammi la man. Cosí un par mio contratta.

V: M'inchino a tant'onor. Pian! Mi fa male.

70. P: (È pur delicatina.) Orsú, le chiavi
Prendi del pan, del vin, della dispensa.
Piú pensiero non vo'. Sí, mia Vespetta,

30. Are everyone's privilege. All women sing and dance.
P: What end, what purpose does that kind of pastime serve?
V: If nothing else, to puff up one's chest.
P: Well said. So you're not in service any more?
V: I asked for my notice and received it.
35. P: (Good news for me.) What was the reason?
V: Oh! I don't wish to speak badly of mistresses.
P: Even so? V: Mine wanted me to take in
Flowers one day, letters the next, portraits the next,
A stream of messages and replies.
40. Don't make me say more. I'm discreet.
P: I understand. Love affairs, wasn't it?
V: I won't say. I think so. But convention
Excuses such a failing and regards love as
An innocent fancy and mere whim.
45. P: But how many fancies does the mistress then have?
V: If I spoke ill of her before,
I must now mention her good side: only six.
But that is unimportant. My mistress didn't always
Look on me with favor.
50. P: How ungrateful! But why? V: Because sometimes,
For instance, in the morning, before she arranged her hair,
I perhaps looked prettier than her.
P: It's a good thing to serve a man on his own.
Isn't that so?   V: If only! Never mind.
55. I did find one, but he was so ugly . . .
P: As ugly as me?   V: What do you mean?
Compared with anyone else
Your Excellency is a jewel, a lily, a sun.
P: (O what nice words!)
Now what do you plan to do? V: Look for a master.
60. P: You'll surely find one. But say: how would you like him to be?
V: For example . . . I'd like . . .
P: (Good looks come in useful!) Well, how do you mean?
V: I'd like him, so to speak, to be . . . your Lordship.
P: Now listen. I live by myself, I'm rich
65. And, listen, generous. If you agree,
I'll make you my maid on the spot.
V: You're jesting with me. (My fortune is made.)
P: Give me your hand. That's how people of my rank do business.
V: I curtsy to such an honor. Go easy! You're hurting me.
70. P: (She's very sensitive.) Arise and take the keys to
The bread, the wine, and the pantry.
My mind is made up. Yes, my Vespetta,

Io mi riposo in te. *V:* Ne vedrà il frutto.
Grazie al Ciel, queste man san far di tutto.

75. *P:* In cittade, in campagna
A tuo piacer far e disfar potrai.
V: E'l salario? *P:* Sarà . . . quel che vorrai.

V: Un padron piú dabben non vidi mai.

[3. Duetto]

P: Nel petto il cor mi giubila.
80. *V:* In sen mi brilla l'anima.
P: Vieni, andiam. *V:* Vada Ella avanti.

P: Vespetta, Vespetta. *V:* No, no, mi
permetta.
P: Lascia, lascia i complimenti.
V: No, no, si contenti.
85. *P:* M'incammino. Tu hai ragion.
V: Illustrissimo padron!
P: Mi sento tutto in gloria.
V: (Affè mi vien da ridere.)
P: Su la man. Qui niun ci osserva.

90. *V:* Troppo onore. Io Le son serva.

P: Tanti inchini non vorrei.
V: Far cosí deggio con Lei.
P: Vieni, vieni. *V:* Vada, vada.

V: (È un gran matto in conclusion.)
95. *P:* O felice Pimpinon. Nel petto, etc.

I'm entrusting myself to you. *V:* You'll reap
the reward.
Thank Heaven, these hands of mine know how
to do everything.

75. *P:* In town and country
You'll be able to do and undo as you please.
V: And my wages? *P:* They'll be . . . whatever
you desire.
V: I never saw such a good master.

[3. Duet]

P: Inside my bosom my heart is rejoicing.
80. *V:* Within my breast my spirit is elated.
P: Come on, let's go. *V:* Please lead the
way.
P: Vespetta, Vespetta. *V:* No, no, allow
me.
P: Have done with compliments.
V: No, no, please accept them.
85. *P:* I'll go in front. You're right.
V: Most excellent master!
P: I feel radiant all over.
V: (Truly, I'm bursting with laughter.)
P: Put your hand over mine. No one's
looking.
90. *V:* You pay me too much honor. I'm your
servant.
P: I don't want so many curtsies.
V: For you I must do it.
P: Come on, come on. *V:* Go ahead, go
ahead.
V: (Really, he's a silly fool.)
95. *P:* O happy Pimpinone. Inside my
bosom, etc.

Intermezzo II

Pimpinone e Vespetta

[4. Recitativo]

P: Vespetta, tu lasciarmi?
V: Tant'è. La mia licenza, o aver piú
ingegno.
P: In che manco? Sai pure . . .
V: Dona di qua; presta di là. Si guarda
100. Meglio la roba sua. Voglio partirmi.

P: Taci, taci. *V:* In rovina andar volete,
E sa il Ciel se mi duol sin nell'interno.

P:(Costei per una casa è un gran
governo.)
Orsú col tuo consiglio; alle mi spese
105. Regola metterò. *V:* No, sinch'avrete
Quelle chiavi alla man, no, no'l farete.

Pimpinone and Vespetta

[4. Recitative]

P: Vespetta, are you leaving me?
V: That's right. Give me my notice, or
show more sense.
P: What have I done wrong? You know . . .
V: Giving here, lending there. You should
look after
100. Your things better. I want to leave.
P: Quiet, quiet. *V:* You want to ruin
yourself,
And Heaven knows how it hurts me
inside.
P: (That lass is a grand housekeeper.)
Out with your advice, then; I'll put my
spending
105. In order. *V:* No, so long as you keep
Those keys in your hands, you won't do it.

P: (Queste son cameriere.) Il ver tu dici.
Prendi: lo scrigno è tuo, ma resta meco.

V: Per servirvi l'accetto. (Egli è pur cieco.)

110. P: Spendi tu stessa, e come piú vorrai.
V: Per vostro ben, non per il mio parlai.
P: (Son fuor d'un bell'imbroglio.)
V: (Questo è cervel.) Da quando in qua le
gioie?
P: Oggi me le comprai con venti scudi.
115. V: Che pazza vanità! Per voi? Vediamo.
Questa è cattiva spesa. Il dissi.
P: Adagio;
E con essa comprai quest'orecchini.
V: O come belli! Il prezzo? P: Ottanta
doppie.
V: Per chi? (Questi son miei!) P: Per te, mio core.

120. V: Per me? Far non si può spesa migliore.

[5. ARIA]

P: Guarda un poco in quest'occhi di foco,
Ed in loro vedrai, mio tesoro,
Che sei di Pimpinon la Pimpinina.
Ti vergogni? Che pensi? Che fai?
125. Guarda, guarda, e guardando saprai
Ch'il mio presente amor è Vespettina. Guarda,
etc.

[6. RECITATIVO]

V: Tacete. Ah, troppo anch'io . . . Non vo'
dir altro.
Vi servo ancor per qualche giorno, e poi . . .

P: Segui. Che poi? Su, parla!
V: Addio. P: Perché?
130. V: Mormora il mondo, e ciarla.
Si dice che voi siete un uom ben fatto,
Io giovinetta, e . . . infin . . . non tanto
brutta.
Ognun vuol dir, quando vuol dir del male.
L'onor mio troppo vale.

135. P: Per far tacere ognun v'è il suo rimedio.

V: Per chi nacque a servir io non lo veggo.

P: Vien qua. Parlo alla buona.
Sei cameriera.   V: È ver, per grazia vostra.

P: E se tu'l vuoi, ti posso far padrona.
140. V: (L'ho colto.) Io sarei ben la fortunata.

P: (Such are maids.) You're right.
Here: the money-box is yours, but stay
with me.
V: I'll agree for your sake. (How blind he
is.)
110. P: You spend as you see fittest.
V: I spoke out for your sake, not mine.
P: (That's got me out of a pretty pickle.)
V: (This is smart.) Since when have you
had those jewels?
P: I bought them today for twenty scudi.
115. V: What crazy indulgence! For you? Look,
That's an extravagance, I'm telling you.
P: Wait;
And I also bought these earrings.
V: O how lovely! How much? P: Eighty
doubloons.
V: For whom? (These are mine!) P: For
you, my darling.
120. V: For me? One can't make a more
sensible purchase.

[5. ARIA]

P: Look into these ardent eyes a little,
And you will see from them, my treasure,
That you are Pimpinone's Pimpinina.
Are you ashamed? What are you thinking?
What are you dong?
125. Look, and by looking you will know
That my present love is Vespetta. Look,
etc.

[6. RECITATIVE]

V: Enough. Ah, I too cannot stop myself
. . . . No more.
I'll serve you for a few more days and
then . . .
P: Go on. And then what? Speak up!
V: Farewell. P: Why?
130. V: The world murmurs and gossips.
People say you're a handsome man,
I'm a young maiden and . . . well . . . not
all that ugly.
The opportunity to speak ill loosens
everyone's tongue.
I value my reputation too much.
135. P: There's a way to make them all keep
quiet.
V: I can't see any for a person born to
service.
P: Come here. I'll speak plainly.
You're a maidservant. V: That's so,
saving your honor.
P: And if you wish, I can make you mistress.
140. V: (I've caught him.) I would indeed be
lucky.

P: (Che buona creatura!) Avrai giudizio?

V: Mi vanto senza inganno e senza vizio.

[7. Aria]

V: Io non sono una di quelle
Nate brutte e fatte belle,
145. E che imparan sul cristallo
A non far un gesto in fallo,
A girar guardi vezzosi,
E a tener la bocca a segno.
Né di quelle vanarelle,
150. Che camminan col compasso,
E si fanno il busto basso
Per mostrar ai piú golosi
Molta roba e poco ingegno. Io, etc.

[8. Recitativo]

P: Cosí va ben. Facciamo i nostri patti.
155. Non vo' concier. V: Io lo depongo or ora.

P: Sul balcon . . . V: Mai non ebbi un tal diletto.

P: Cene, teatri e balli . . . V: Io non li bramo.

P: Giochi e veglie . . .   V: Il mio genio è solitario.

P: Libri amorosi . . . V: Io leggerò il lunario.

160. P: Maschera . . . V: Non so dir cos'ella sia.

P: Feste d'orsi e di tori . . . V: In casa mia.

P: Sei mia sposa. V: Sua serva in ogni stato.
Ma senza dote . . . (Egli vi pensa, è fatta.)

P: Io te la fo di dieci mila. Andiamo.
165. Oh! Mi scordava il meglio. Io non
       permetto
Visite, convenienze e complimenti.
V: Intendo, e ubbidirò. P: Lieto son io.
V: (Prometto al suo piacer per fare il mio.)

[9. Duetto]

P: Stendi, stendi. Uh, che allegrezza!
170. V: Prendi, prendi, Oh, che fortuna!
P: (Che bel tratto.) V: (È pur matto!)
P: Fammi un vezzo. V: Mio Cupido.
P: (Non v'è prezzo.) V: (Me ne rido.)

P: Cara sposa, ⎫
V: Dolce sposo, ⎬ sí, a goder.

P: (What a good creature!) You'll be
sensible?

V: I pride myself on being without guile
or vice.

[7. Aria]

V: I'm not one of those
Born ugly and made pretty,
145. And who learn in front of the mirror
Not to make a false movement,
To throw amorous glances,
And choose their words cleverly.
Nor one of those vain women
150. Who walk ever so carefully
And sport a low neckline
To reveal to greedy-eyed men
Plenty of merchandise but little sense.
I'm not, etc.

[8. Recitative]

P: That's fine. Let's settle our terms.
155. I want no later changes. V: I promise
here and now.
P: On the balcony . . . V: I've never
had that pleasure.
P: Suppers, theaters, and balls . . . V: I've
no interest in them.
P: Card games and parties . . . V: I'm
solitary by nature.
P: Books about love . . . V: I'll read the
calendar.
160. P: Wearing a mask . . . V: I don't know what
that is.
P: Bear-baiting and bullfights . . . V: I'll stay at
home.
P: You're my wife. V: Your servant, whatever
my state.
But I've no dowry . . . (He's thinking about
it, it's done.)
P: I'll make it ten thousand for you. Let's go.
165. Oh! I forgot the most important condition. I don't
allow visits, social gatherings, and admirers.

V: I understand and will obey. P: I'm pleased.
V: (I'm promising to please him for the sake of my
own pleasure.)

[9. Duet]

P: Give me your hand. Ooh, what rapture!
170. V: Here it is. Oh, what luck!
P: (What a catch.) V: (He's crazy!)
P: Give me a cuddle. V: My Cupid.
P: (This is beyond price.) V: (What a
laugh.)

P: Dear wife, ⎫
V: Dear husband, ⎬ let's away to pleasure.

175. V: (Tanto brutto ⎱ P: (Tal bellezza ⎱
Non v'è alcun.) ⎰ Non l'ha nessuna.) ⎰
V: (È pur cotto, il sempliciotto.)
P: (Per amore manca il core.)
V: Parla, o caro. P: Parla, o cara.
180. V: ⎱
P: ⎰ M'impedisce il gran piacer.
V: Ora è il tempo del goder. Stendi, etc.

175. V: (There's no one ⎱   P: (There's no one ⎱
So ugly.)   ⎰   So fair.)   ⎰
V: (He's madly in love, the silly old fool.)
P: (Love is making my heart stop beating.)
V: Speak, my dearest. P: Speak, my angel.
180. V: ⎱
P: ⎰ My great delight prevents me.
V: Now's the time for pleasure. Give me, etc.

Intermezzo III

Vespetta e Pimpinone

[10. RECITATIVO]

V: Io vado ove mi piace. Oh, questa è
bella!
P: (Oh, questa è brutta!) Io vo' saperlo
adesso.
V: Deggio render ragion d'ogni mio
passo?
185. P: Son marito. V:Hai ragione. Io vado a spasso.

P: A spasso? È questo il patto?

V: Diran che siete matto. A saggia moglie
Non si fan questi conti, e un buon marito,
S'ella è dabben, di lei si fida e tace.

190. P: Voglio saper . . . V: Noi non staremo in pace.
P: Vespetta . . . V: Pimpinone . . . (Ei si rimette.)

P: (O che flemma vi vuol! Che feci mai?)

V: Per aver libertà mi maritai.
Compagne son le mogli, e non già
schiave.
195. P: È ver. Ma infin . . . Vespetta . . .
V: Piú di creanza. Un poco di "Signora."

P: Illustrissima, sí. (Son in malora.)
V: (Cosí si fa.) La voglio a modo mio.

P: Andiamo, sí. Con voi ne vengo anch'io.
200. V: Oh, questo no! Voglio andar sola.
Addio.
P: Almen dite ove andate.
V: Vado a passar il dí da mia comare.

P: Andate, se volete;
Ma dite mal di me men che potete.

Vespetta and Pimpinone

[10. RECITATIVE]

V: I can go where I please. Oh, this is nice!

P: (Oh, this is horrible!) I want an answer
now.
V: Do I have to account for every step I
make?
185. P: I'm your husband. V: So you are.
I'm going out to amuse myself.
P: To amuse yourself? Is that what we
agreed?
V: People will say you are mad. No one talks
like that
To a virtuous wife, and a good husband
Trusts her, if she's respectable and shuts
up.
190. P: I want to know . . .   V: We'll have no peace.
P: Vespetta . . . V: Pimpinone . . . (He's start-
ing again.)
P: (O what restraint one needs! Whatever
did I do?)
V: I got married to enjoy some freedom.
Wives are companions, not slaves.

195. P: That's true. But really . . . Vespetta . . .
V: Show more politeness. How about calling
me "Madam."
P: Yes, my Lady. (I'm in a bad way.)
V: (That's the style.) I like to do things my
way.
P: Let's go, then. I'm coming with you.
200. V: Oh no you're not! I want to go alone.
Good bye.
P: At least tell me where you're going.
V: I'm off to spend the day with my lady
friend.
P: Go if you want to;
But don't speak badly of me any more
than you need.

[11. Aria]

205. *P*: So quel che si dice, e quel che si fa:
"Sustrissima, Sustrissima, come si sta?"
"Bene." E poi subito: "Quel mio marito
È pur stravagante, è pur indiscreto.
Pretende che in casa io stia tutto il dí."
210. E l'altra risponde: "Gran bestia ch'egl'è.
Prendete, comare, l'esempio da me.
Voleva anch'il mio. Ma l'ho ben chiarito.
Di far a mio modo trovato ho il segreto:
S'ei dice di no, io dico di sí." So quel, etc.

[12. Recitativo]

215. *P*: Per questa volta andate,
Ma presto ritornate.
V: Del "presto" non m'impegno. Infino a
sera.
P: Di notte per le strade?
V: Di grazia che qualcun non mi rubasse.

220. *P*: Maledetto quel dí . . .
V: Maledirmi? Insolente!
P: Maledico il dolor ch'ho in questo dente.
Vada, vada, ma senti . . . Ella mi senta.
Per l'avvenir vorrei
225. Piú governo alla casa, e men d'orgoglio.

V: Rispondo al tuo "vorrei" con il mio
"voglio."
Il teatro, la veglia, il gioco, il ballo,
La visita, la maschera, il balcone:
Tutto è per me. M'intendi?
230. *P*: (Il genio solitario.) Promettesti . . .
V: Lo so e no'l so. Promisi e non promisi.

P: Che saresti con me . . . Guardami.
Ascolta.
Nemica delle pompe, e sempre buona.

V: In quel tempo ero serva: or son
padrona.

[13. Aria]

235. *V*: Voglio far come fan l'altre,
Ben danzar, parlar francese,
Star in gala, esser cortese,
Ma però con l'onestà.
Voglio anch'io saper cos'è
240. La maniglia e la spadiglia,
E chiamar o l'asso o il re,
Quando il punto mi dirà. Voglio, etc.

[11. Aria]

205. *P*: I know what they say, I know what
they do:
"My lady, my lady, how are things?"
"Splendid." And then it starts: "This
husband of mine
Is really eccentric, really inquisitive.
He expects me to stay at home all day
long."
210. And the other replies: "What a great brute
he is.
Take a lesson from me, my friend.
Mine wanted to do the same. But I put
him straight.
I've found the secret of doing things my
way:
If he says no, I say yes." I know, etc.

[12. Recitative]

215. *P*: This time you can go,
But come back soon.
V: I can't promise "soon." Until this
evening!
P: Out on the streets at nighttime?
V: Little chance that anyone would rob
me.

220. *P*: I curse the day . . .
V: Cursing me? What impudence!
P: I'm cursing the pain I have in this
tooth.
Go, go, but listen . . . Please listen.
I'd like you in the future
225. To attend more to the home and act less
haughtily.
V: My reply to your "I'd like" is my own
"I want."
The theater, parties, card games, dancing,
Visiting, wearing a mask, the balcony:
These are all for me. Understand?
230. *P*: (Solitary by nature.) You promised . . .
V: I know and I don't know. I promised
and I didn't promise.
P: That with me you would be . . . Look
at me. Listen.
Averse to outward show and always
good-humored.
V: Then I was a servant: now I am a
mistress.

[13. Aria]

235. *V*: I want to do as the others do,
Dance well, speak French,
Dress up, be flirtatious,
But with decorum, however.
I too want to know what
240. The *manilla* and the *spadilla* are,
And to call the ace or the king
When my turn arrives. I want, etc.

[14. Recitativo]

P: Ma s'io giocassi, e che diresti allora?

V: Tu'l faresti per vizio, io per diletto.
245. Non si può! Quella roba è roba mia.

P: (Buono.) Se tanto spendessi in
    frascherie?
V: Bel veder. Sei un uom. Tutto ti basta.
Moda e galanteria son per le donne.

P: E s'io facessi un dí che con le mogli
250. L'adoprare il baston fosse alla moda?
V: Bastone a una mia pari? In questo
    punto
Ti protesto il divorzio. I dieci mila,
N'ho qui la carta, io t'addimando adesso.

P: (Misero me.) Scherzai.
255. V: Baston? Viver cosí piú non si puote.
O la mia libertade o la mia dote!
P: (Che deggio far? Ne sono innamorato,
Ed essa ben lo sa.) Fa quel che brami.

V: (Ho vinto il punto.) Se mai piú mi parli
260. In guisa tal . . . villano . . .

P: Sí, Vespettina mia, fa quel che brami.

V: Voglio cavarti il cor. P: (Uomini, a voi.)

V: Quel che so far, bell'umorin, vedrete.
Basta: te n'avvedrai.
    P: (Donne, ridete.)

[15. Duetto]

265. V: Se mai piú . . . P: (Sia maledetto . . .)
V: Che! Che dici? P: Niente, niente.

V: Se mai piú noi la vedremo,
Romperemo il matrimonio.
P: (Maledetto quando mai
270. M'intricai con tal demonio.)
V: Fai piú il bravo?
    P: Ti son schiavo.
V: (Che diletto!) P: (Che dispetto!)
V: Già lo sai, vo' libertà.
P: Tu l'avrai. Va pur, va, va.
275. V: (Un gran punto ho guadagnato.)
P: (Son confuso e disperato.)
V: Parla su! P: Mi duole il dente.
V: Se mai piú . . . Baston con me?
P: Fa pur su, dubbio non c'è.
280. V: Ti saprò romper la testa.
P: Mi vorrebbe ancora questa.
Chi ha le mogli indiavolate
Presto affè si pentirà. Se mai, etc.

[14. Recitative]

P: But if I played cards, what would you
    then say?
V: In you it would be a vice, in me a
    pastime.
245. No you don't! Those things are mine.
P: (Good.) If I spent as much on
    fripperies?
V: A fine sight that would be. You're a
    man. Anything does for you.
Fashion and style are for ladies.
P: And if one day I decided that taking
250. A stick to one's wife was fashionable?
V: A stick to someone like me? I would
    then
Demand a divorce. Now give me back my
    ten thousand,
I have the deed here.
P: (Poor me.) I was joking.
255. V: A stick? I can't live like this any more.
My freedom, or my dowry!
P: (What can I do? I'm in love with her,
And she knows it very well.) Do as you
    wish.
V: (I've won the point.) If you ever
    address me
260. Like that again . . . you boor . . .
P: Yes, Vespetta, my dear, do as you
    wish.
V: I want to tear out your heart. P: (Over to you,
    men.)
V: What I can do, you witty man, you will
    soon see.
Enough: you will learn. P: (Laugh, ladies.)

[15. Duet]

265. V: If ever again . . . P: (Cursed be . . .)
V: What! What are you saying? P: Nothing,
    nothing.
V: If we ever quarrel like this again,
That will be the end of our marriage.
P: (Cursed be the day when
270. I got involved with such a devil.)
V: Will you behave yourself in the future?
    P: I'm your servant.
V: (What bliss!) P: (What vexation!)
V: You know it already. I want freedom.
P: You'll have it. Just go, go.
275. V: (I've won a great point.)
P: (I'm confused and desperate.)
V: Speak up! P: My tooth aches.
V: If ever again . . . A stick to me?
P: Just carry on, there's no doubt of that.
280. V: I'll know how to bash you on the head.
P: That would be the last straw.
He whose wife is possessed by a devil
Will indeed soon regret it. If ever, etc.

Appendix

Pimpinone: The Productions

Pariati's libretto was set by three different composers (Albinoni, Conti, and Telemann), and it remained in production for at least thirty-two years. This section lists all of the known eighteenth-century productions of *Pimpinone* in chronological order and documents as many details of each performance as possible.

Students of baroque opera have to rely heavily on published libretti for basic data concerning specific productions. Thus it is unfortunate that the libretti of comic intermezzi, particularly intermezzi of the first generation (from 1706 to ca. 1720), often lack information of the type regularly found in opera libretti: the names of the composer and the librettist are almost always missing. Although these names sometimes appear in the libretto of the opera with which the intermezzi was performed, to establish the identity of that opera in the first place can be difficult, since this is a matter on which the libretti of intermezzi are so often silent—sometimes for the good reason that the same production migrated from one opera to another during one season.[1]

Fortunately, however, the missing information can often be obtained or deduced by other means. Sometimes, opera libretti reveal the identity of the intermezzi with which they were performed by means of a cast list that gives not only the names, but also the roles of the comic singers. In other cases the libretti of an opera and the set of intermezzi associated with it are preserved in a common binding, a strong (but not conclusive) indication that they were performed together. It may also happen that only one opera was performed at the same theater as the intermezzi during the season in question. For information concerning Venetian productions, another aid exists. Whereas the published opera catalog of Antonio Groppo,[2] like that of Gian Carlo Bonlini before him,[3] does not list intermezzi, a manuscript catalog initially drawn up by Groppo in 1741 and continued until 1767 includes them.[4] This less well known register, which seems to be an example of a "Catalogo in 4. magno M.S. che imita la Stampa" advertised in Bonlini's published catalog,[5] is particularly valuable for its inclusion of information derived from sources other than libretti.

A list of the twenty-nine known productions of *Pimpinone* between 1708 and 1740 (the year of the last known production) follows. Because the three extant sources for the music have been described above (see p. xi), this list concerns itself only with the libretti associated with the various productions. Each entry contains, where information is available, the following details: (a) the *year* of the production, followed by a letter to distinguish that production from others in the same year; (b) the *season* and/or *date* of the first performance;[6] (c) the *city* and *theater*; (d) the *opera* or other stage work with which the set of intermezzi was performed, with the names of the librettist and composer; (e) the names of the *singers* playing Vespetta and Pimpinone, respectively;[7] (f) indication of whether the libretto exists as a separate bibliographic entity or is combined with that of the opera; (g) the pagination of the libretto or (if unpaginated) the number of pages, excluding blanks; (h) locations for the libretto of *Pimpinone* (see below for list of library sigla); (i) locations for the libretto of the opera with which *Pimpinone* was performed; (j) transcription of the *title page* or (when there is no title page) the heading of Intermezzo I; (k) reference to the Selected Bibliography (see p. xxvii);[8] (l) additional remarks.

Library sigla

BELGIUM (B)

Bc	Brussels, Conservatoire Royal de Musique

CANADA (C)

Tu	Toronto, University Library

FRANCE (F)

Pn	Paris, Bibliothèque Nationale

GERMANY (D, BRD)

B	Berlin (West), Staatsbibliothek der Stiftung Preussischer Kulturbesitz
W	Wolfenbüttel, Herzog-August-Bibliothek

GREAT BRITAIN (GB)

Lwi	London, Warburg Institute

ITALY (I)

Bc	Bologna, Civico Museo Bibliografico Musicale
Bu	Bologna, Biblioteca Universitaria

FAN	Fano, Biblioteca Comunale Federiciana
Mb	Milan, Biblioteca Nazionale Braidense
Mc	Milan, Conservatorio di Musica Giuseppe Verdi
MAC	Macerata, Biblioteca Comunale Mozzi-Borgetti
PAc	Parma, Biblioteca Palatina (Conservatorio)
Rsc	Rome, Conservatorio di Musica Santa Cecilia
Rn	Rome, Biblioteca Nazionale Centrale Vittorio Emanuele II
Tco	Turin, Conservatorio Statale di Musica G. Verdi
UDc	Udine, Biblioteca Civica Vincenzo Joppi
Vcg	Venice, Casa di Goldoni
Vgc	Venice, Fondazione Giorgio Cini
Vnm	Venice, Biblioteca Nazionale Marciana

SPAIN (E)

Mn	Madrid, Biblioteca Nacional

UNITED STATES (US)

BEu	Berkeley, University of California Music Library
Wc	Washington, Library of Congress

YUGOSLAVIA (YU)

Lnm	Ljubljana, Knjižnica Narodnega Muzeja
Lsk	Ljubljana, Slovanska Knjižnica

Selected Bibliography

Allacci, Lione. *Drammaturgia di Lione Allacci accresciuta e continuata fino all'anno MDCCLV*. Venice, 1755.

Cinelli, Carlo. *Memorie cronistoriche del teatro di Pesaro dall'anno 1637 al 1897*. Pesaro, 1898.

Cvetko, Dragotin. *Musikgeschichte der Südslawen*. Kassel-Ljubljana, 1975.

Gandini, Alessandro. *Cronistoria dei teatri di Modena dal 1539 al 1871*. 3 vols. Modena, 1873.

Giazotto, Remo. *Tomaso Albinoni*. Milan, 1945.

Groppo, Antonio. *Catalogo purgatissimo di tutti li drammi per musica recitatisi ne' teatri di Venezia dall'anno MDCXXXVII sin oggi* (MS, Venice, Biblioteca Nazionale Marciana, Cod. It.–VII–2326 [=8263], 1741–1767).

Haas, Robert. "Die Musik in der Wiener deutschen Stegreifkomödie." *Studien zur Musikwissenschaft* XII (1925): 3–64.

Hadamowsky, Franz. *Barocktheater am Wiener Kaiserhof*. Vienna, 1955.

Kirkendale, Ursula. *Antonio Caldara. Sein Leben und seine venezianisch-römischen Oratorien*. Graz-Cologne, 1966.

Kirkendale, Ursula, and Kirkendale, Warren. "Caldara, Antonio." In *Dizionario biografico degli italiani*, XVI: 556–566. Rome, 1973.

Lazarevich, Gordana. "The Role of the Neapolitan Intermezzo in the Evolution of Eighteenth-Century Musical Style: Literary, Symphonic and Dramatic Aspects 1685–1735." Ph. D. dissertation, Columbia University, 1970.

Loewenberg, Alfred. *Annals of Opera 1597–1940*. 3rd ed. London, 1978.

Mamczarz, Irène. *Les intermèdes comiques italiens au XVIIIe siècle en France et en Italie*. Paris, 1972.

Maertens, Willi. "Georg Philipp Telemann und seine Interpreten Margaretha Susanna und Johann Kayser." Edited by Günther Fleischhauer, Wolf Hobohm, and Willi Maertens. *Telemann-Renaissance. Werk und Wiedergabe*. Magdeburg, 1973, pp. 68–85.

Mooser, Robert-Aloys. *Annales de la musique et des musiciens en Russie au XVIIIe siècle*. 3 vols. Geneva, 1948–1951.

Pellegrini, Almachilde. *Spettacoli lucchesi nei secoli XVII–XIX*. Lucca, 1914.

Ricci, Corrado. *I teatri di Bologna nei secoli XVII e XVIII*. Bologna, 1888.

Schmidt, Gustav Friedrich. *Chronologisches Verzeichnis der in Wolfenbüttel, Braunschweig, Salzthal, Bevern und Blankenburg aufgeführten Opern, Ballette und Schauspiele (Komödien) mit Musik bis zur Mitte des 18. Jahrhunderts nach den vorhandenen Textbüchern, Partituren und nach anderen gedruckten und handschriftlichen Quellenurkunden*. Munich, 1929.

Škerlj, Stanko. *Italijansko gledališče v Ljubljani v preteklih stoletjih*. Ljubljana, 1973.

Sonneck, Oscar G. *Catalogue of Opera Librettos printed before 1800*. 2 vols. Washington, D.C., 1914.

Strohm, Reinhard. *Italienische Opernarien des frühen Settecento (1720–1730)*. 2 vols. Cologne, 1976.

Troy, Charles E. *The Comic Intermezzo: A Study in the History of Eighteenth-Century Italian Opera*. Ann Arbor, 1979.

Weaver, Robert L., and Weaver, Norma W. *A Chronology of Music in the Florentine Theater 1590–1750. Operas, Prologues, Finales, Intermezzos and Plays with Incidental Music*. Detroit, 1978.

Werner, Theodor W. "Zum Neudruck von G. Ph. Telemanns 'Pimpinone' in den Reichsdenkmalen." *Archiv für Musikforschung* I (1936): 361–365.

Wolff, Hellmuth Christian. *Die Barockoper in Hamburg (1678–1738)*. 2 vols. Wolfenbüttel, 1957.

List of Productions

1. (a) 1708a (b) autumn, 26 November (c) Venice, S. Cassiano (d) *Astarto* (Zeno and Pariati/Albinoni) (e)

Santa Marchesini, Giovanni Battista Cavana (f) separate (g) 1–12 (h) E-Mn, F-Pn, I-Bc, I-PAc, I-Rsc, I-Mb, I-Vcg, US-Wc (i) I-Bc, US-Wc (j) PIMPINONE / INTERMEZZI / Comici Musicali / Da rappresentarsi nel Teatro / Tron di S. Cassano [sic] / L'Autunno dell'anno MDCCVIII. / IN VENEZIA, MDCCVIII. / Appresso Marino Rossetti. / In Merceria, all'Insegna della Pace. / Con Licenza de' Superiori, e Privilegio. (k) Allacci; Groppo (l) Groppo, p. 161, records that *Pimpinone* continued to be performed, with the same cast, during performances of *Il falso Tiberino* (Zeno and Pariati/ C. F. Pollarolo) at S. Cassiano in carnival 1709. The libretto was not reprinted. Mamczarz's report (p. 453) of a production at S. Cassiano in autumn 1709 is unsubstantiated.

2. (a) 1709a (b) *inverno*, 4 November [name-day of the Archduke Charles] (c) Naples, Royal Palace and subsequently S. Bartolomeo (d) *Engelberta* (Zeno and Pariati/Orefici and Mancini) (f) combined (g) 61–72 (i) I-Bc, I-Bu (j) INTERMEZZO / PRIMO./ Vespetta, e Pimpinone. (k) Haas; Strohm; Wolff.

3. (a) 1709b (c) Milan? (f) separate (g) 1–16 (h) I-Mc (j) PIMPINONE / INTERMEZZI / MVSICALI./ IN MILANO, 1709. / Per Francesco Vigone, e fratelli. / Con licenza de' Superiori. (l) It is not certain that Milan was the place of performance, as Milanese printers commonly served other localities.

4. (a) 1711a (b) carnival, 9 February (c) Rome, Teatro Domestico del Principe di Cerveteri (d) *La costanza in amore vince l'inganno* (librettist unknown / Caldara) (e) Annibale Pio Fabbri, Giovanni Battista Cavana (f) combined (g) 21–24, 41–44, 65–68 (i) I-MAC, I-Vgc [Act I/Intermezzo I only] (j) INTERMEDIO PRIMO. / Cortile con Colonnate./ Vespetta, e Pimpinone. (k) Kirkendale, U.; Kirkendale, U., and Kirkendale, W. (l) Since female singers were excluded from the Roman stage, the role of Vespetta had to be taken by a male singer. The celebrated Bolognese tenor Annibale Pio Fabbri (1697–1760) was evidently still young enough to sing an alto part! Kirkendale and Kirkendale, col. 562, imply that *Pimpinone* was performed with *La costanza in amore* in Macerata at the end of 1710. See also Kirkendale, U., pp. 364–365.

5. (a) 1711b (b) *fiera*, May (c) Ferrara, S. Stefano (d) *La fede tradita e vendicata* (Silvani/F. Gasparini) (e) Rosa Ungarelli, Giovanni Battista Cavana (f) separate (g) 1–15 (h) B-Bc, I-Mb, (i) B-Bc, GB-Lwi, I-Bc (j) PIMPINONE / E / VESPETTA. / INTERMEZZO PRIMO. [colophon] IN FERRARA / M.DCC.XI. / Per Bernardino Barbie / Con lic. de' Super (k) Troy (l) The partnership of Ungarelli and Cavana in this production is perhaps, as Troy (p. 49) suggests, the route by which the repertory of Cavana and his earlier partners (in particular, Santa Marchesini) passed to Ungarelli and her subsequent partners (notably Antonio Ristorini).

6. (a) 1712a (b) *fiera*, May (c) Vicenza, Teatro delle Grazie (d) *Peribea in Salamina* (librettist unknown / C. F. Pollarolo) (e) Santa Marchesini, Giovanni Battista Cavana (f) separate (g) 1–12 (h) I-Mb (i) I-Mb (j) PIMPINONE / INTERMEZZI / Comici Musicali / Da rappresentarsi nel Nuouo / Teatro delle Gratie / DI VICENZA / Il Maggio 1712 / IN VICENZA, MDCCXII./ Per Tomaso Lauezari / Con licenza de' Superiori. (k) Troy (l) A production of 1712 at Padua, not Vicenza, is noted by Troy (p. 152). This appears to be an error and may stem from the fact that the libretto of *Peribea* for the same production was first published by Penada in Padua (examples in I-Mb, I-Vnm, and elsewhere) before being reprinted by Lavezari with one change in the cast list.

7. (a) 1713a (b) carnival, 26 December 1712 (c) Florence, Teatro di via del Cocomero (d) *Il tiranno eroe* (Cassani/Albinoni?) (e) Anna Maria Bianchi, Filippo Rossi (f) libretto not traced, probably not published (i) I-Mb, I-Rn, I-Vnm, US-BEu (k) Weaver and Weaver.

8. (a) 1714a (b) carnival (c) Parma, Teatro Ducale (d) *La fede nei tradimenti* (Gigli/composer unknown) (e) Rosa Ungarelli, Angelo Cantelli (f) separate (g) 1–14 (h) I-Bc (j) INTERMEZZI / DI / VESPETTA, E PIMPINONE / RAPPRESENTATI / NELL'OPERA / INTITOLATA / LA FEDE / NE' TRADIMENTI / Il Carnevale dell'Anno 1714. / IN PARMA, / Per Giuseppe Rosati./ CON LICENZA DE' SUPERIORI. (l) Mamczarz, p. 213, notes that the intermezzi of *Pimpinone* were the first examples of the genre performed at the Teatro Ducale.

9. (a) 1714b (b) autumn (c) Modena, Teatro Molza (d) *Il Radamisto* (unidentified librettist and composer) (e) Angelica Trebbi?, Giovanni Battista Cavana (i) I-Bc (k) Gandini (l) According to Gandini (I: 51), *Pimpinone* was performed with *Il Radamisto*. However, the example of the *Radamisto* libretto cited by Gandini (Bologna, Civico Museo Bibliografico Musicale, 7014a) has the intermezzi for the characters Lisetta and Astrobolo appended, and not *Pimpinone*. On this point the published catalog of the library is also in error. The existence of this may therefore be doubted.

10. (a) 1715a (c) Udine, Teatro Mantica (f) separate (g) 1–12 (h) I-Mb, I-UDc (j) PIMPJNONE / Intermezzi / Comici Musicali / Da recitarsi nel famosissimo / Teatro MANTICA IN / UDINE l'Anno / 1715. / IN UDJNE / Gio: Domenico Murero / Con Licenza de' Superiori.

11. (a) 1716a (b) carnival (c) Turin, Teatro del Principe di Carignano (d) *Arideno* (Molina/Fiorè) (e) Rosa Ungarelli, Antonio Ristorini (f) separate (g) 1–17 (h) B-Bc, I-Tco (i) B-Bc (j) INTERMEZZI / COMICI-MUSICALI / DI VESPETTA, E PIMPINONE. / Da rappresentarsi in Torino / Dalla Signora ROSA UNGARELLI, e Sig. ANTONIO RISTORINI, / Nel Drama intitolato: / L'ARIDENO / Nel Carnovale 1716. / IN TORINO / Per Gio.

Francesco Mairesse, e Giovanni Radix / Stampatori dell'Illᵐa Accad. degl'Innominati / di Bra, all'insegna di S. Teresa. / Con lic. de' Superiori. (k) Troy (l) Troy (p. 50) records this production as the earliest one to feature the Ungarelli-Ristorini partnership.

12. (a) 1717a (b) carnival, 24 January (c) Vienna, Court Theater (d) *Sesostri, re di Egitto* (Pariati/Conti) (e) Faustina Bordoni, Pietro Paolo Pezzoni (f) combined (g) 69–90 (i) US-Wc (j) INTERMEZZO PRIMO. / Grilletta, e Pimpinone. (k) Haas; Hadamowsky (l) Setting by F. Conti. In the version of the libretto used for this setting and production, the part of Vespetta is renamed Griletta.

13. (a) 1717b (b) *primavera* (c) Bologna, Teatro Formagliari (d) *Lucio Vero* (Zeno/Perti?) (e) Rosa Ungarelli, Antonio Ristorini (f) separate (g) 1–16 (h) I-Bc (i) I-Bc (j) INTERMEZZI / E / MUTAZIONI D'ARIE / NEL DRAMA INTITOLATO / LUCIO VERO. / LA SERVA ASTUTA / VESPETTA, E PIMPINONE. / SIGNORA ROSA UNGARELLI. / E / SIGNOR ANTONIO RISTORINI. / IN BOLOGNA. MDCCXVII. / Per li Successori del Benacci. Con lic. de' Super. (k) Ricci (l) First performance under the title *La serva astuta* (cf. 1725c, 1728a).

14. (a) 1718a (c) Florence, Teatro alla Pergola (e) Rosa Ungarelli?, Antonio Ristorini (f) separate (g) 1–16 (h) I-Rn (j) INTERMEZZI / DI / VESPETTA, E PIMPINONE / PER IL DRAMA, CHE SI RAPPRESENTA IN FIRENZE / Nel Teatro degl'Illustriss. SS. Accademici Immobili / posto in Via della Pergola / SOTTO LA PROTEZIONE / DELL'ALTEZZA REALE / DEL SERENISSIMO / GIO: GASTONE / GRAN PRINCIPE DI TOSCANA. / IN FIRENZE, MDCCXVIII. / Da Anton Maria Albizzini: da S. Maria in Campo. / Con Licenza de' Superiori. (k) Weaver and Weaver.

15. (a) 1718b (c) Fano, Teatro della Fortuna (d) *Il tradimento traditor di se stesso* (Silvani?/Lotti?) (e) Giovanni Battista Perugini, Domenico Manzi (h) I-FAN (l) The libretto, which the present writer has not inspected, is recorded in the card index of the Ufficio Ricerca Fondi Musicali, Milan.

16. (a) 1720a (b) August (c) Brunswick (d) *Sesostri, re di Egitto* (Pariati/Conti) (k) Schmidt (l) Setting as 1717a.

17. (a) 1722a (b) 24 October (c) Munich, Court Theater (d) *I veri amici* (Silvani, revised Lalli/Albinoni) (e) Rosa Ungarelli, Antonio Ristorini (f) separate (g) 1–16 (h) BRD-W, US-Wc (i) BRD-W (j) VESPETTA / E / PIMPINONE. / INTERMEZZI / COMICI MUSICALI. / Da Rappresentarsi la Prima volta, che si esibisce / il Drama. (k) Giazotto.

18. (a) 1723a (b) carnival (c) Pesaro, Teatro del Sole (f) separate (k) Cinelli.

19. (a) 1724a (b) *primavera* (c) Parma, Court Theater (d)

Il Venceslao (Zeno/Capello) (e) Rosa Ungarelli, Antonio Ristorini (f) separate (g) 1–14 (h) C-Tu (i) C-Tu (j) C-Tu, I-Bc (j) INTERMEZZI / DI / VESPETTA, E PIMPINONE / RAPPRESENTATI / NELL'OPERA / INTITOLATA / IL VENCESLAO / NELLA PRIMAVERA 1724 / IN PARMA, / Per Giuseppe Rosati / CON LICENZA DE' SUPERIORI.

20. (a) 1724b (b) carnival (c) Lucca, S. Girolamo (d) *Lucio Papirio* (Salvi/various unidentified composers) and/or *Rodelinda* (librettist unknown / Canuti) (e) Maria Giovanna Pioli, Pietro Pertici (k) Pellegrini.

21. (a) 1725a (b) carnival (c) Venice, S. Moise (d) *Li sdegni cangiati in amore* (Silvani/Buini) (f) separate [two editions] (g) 1–12 [both editions] (h) I-Rsc [Edition 1], I-Vnm [Edition 2] (i) I-Bc, I-Vgc (j) 1. PIMPINONE / INTERMEZZI / DA RAPPRESENTARSI / Nel Teatro Giustiniano / di S. Moisè. / Il Carnevale dell'anno MDCXXV. / In VENEZIA, / Appresso Marino Rossetti, in Merceria / all'insegna della Pace. / Con Licenza de' Superiori. 2. PIMPINONE / INTERMEZZI / DA RAPPRESENTARSI / IN MUSICA. / Con Licenza de' Superiori. (l) The title-page of Edition 2 contains a handwritten note in a contemporary hand, linking this production with *Li sdegni cangiati in amore*.

22. (a) 1725b (b) 27 September (c) Hamburg, Gänsemarkt ("Hamburger Theater") (d) *Tamerlano* (Haym, arranged J. P. Praetorius/Handel) (f) separate (g) 1–16 (h) US-Wc (i) US-Wc (j) Die ungleiche Heyrath / Zwischen / VESPETTA / Und PIMPINONE, / In dreyen INTERMEDIIS / Auf dem / Hamburger THEATRO / Vorgestellt. (k) Loewenberg; Sonneck; Werner; Wolff. (l) Setting by G. P. Telemann. The text, revised by J. P. Praetorius, is based on that of the libretto of 1725a: the recitatives are in a German paraphrase; the original arias are left in Italian, but Praetorius has added three numbers (an aria and two duets) in German. Contrary to Loewenberg's suggestion (col. 152), Telemann's setting owes nothing to Albinoni's original.

23. (a) 1725c (b) autumn (c) S. Giovanni in Persiceto, Teatro de' Signori Accademici Candidi Uniti (e) Antonia Bertelli, Pellegrino Gaggiotti (f) separate (g) 1–16 (h) I-Vgc (j) LA SERVA / ASTUTA / Intermezzi in Musica / Da rappresentarsi / NEL TEATRO DE' SIGNORI ACCADEMICI / CANDIDI UNITI / IN S. GIO: IN PERSICETO / L'Autunno dell'Anno / MDCCXXV. / In Bologna per Lelio dalla Volpe. / Con licenza de' Superiori.

24. (a) 1728a (b) carnival (c) Bologna, Teatro Marsigli Rossi (d) *Il Malmocor* (Buini/Buini) (e) Maria Penna, Pellegrino Gaggiotti (f) separate (g) 1–14 (h) I-Bc (i) I-Bc (j) LA SERVA / ASTUTA / Intermezzi in Musica / Da rappresentarsi / NEL TEATRO / MARSIGLJ ROSSI / Il Carnovale dell'Anno 1728. (k) Ricci.

25. (a) 1728b (b) 29 August (c) Brussels, Théâtre de la

Monnaie (d) *Griselda* (Zeno/Orlandini) (e) Rosa Ungarelli, Antonio Ristorini (f) separate (h) formerly B-Bc, now lost (i) B-Bc (k) Lazarevich; Mamczarz; Strohm; Troy.

26. (a) 1730a (c) Hamburg, Gänsemarkt ("Schau-Platz") (d) *Mistevojus, König der Obotriten oder Wenden* (Müller/Keiser) (e) Margaretha Susanna Kayser, Johann Gottfried Riemenschneider (f) separate (g) 20 pp. (h) D-B (j) Die / Ungleiche Heyrath / Oder das / Herrsch = süchtige Cammer = Mädgen. / In einem schertzhafften / Zwischen = Spiele / Auf dem / Hamburgischen / Schau = Platz / Aufgeführet. / Gredruckt mit Stromerischen Schrifften (k) Maertens; Werner; Wolff (1) Wolff (vol. I: 117n) gives 1740 as the libretto's date of publication. The text is unaltered from that of 1725b, and a preface confirms Telemann's authorship of the music.

27. (a) 1731a (b) August (c) Brunswick (d) *Cyrus und Tomyris oder Hass und Liebe* (Noris, revised Rolli, transl. unknown/G. Bononcini?) (k) Schmidt (1) Setting as 1717a.

28. (a) 1731b (b) 18 March (c) Moscow, Court Theater (d) *Le cocu imaginaire* [18 March] and *L'amant trahi* [3 April]; both spoken comedies (e) Margherita Ermini, Cosimo Ermini (k) Mooser.

29. (a) 1740a (b) carnival (c) Ljubljana, Provincial Palace (d) *Artaserse* (Metastasio/Hasse) and/or *Rosmira* (Stampiglia/Hasse?) (e) Antonia Bertelli, Giovanni Michieli (f) separate (g) 35 pp. (h) I-Bc (j) both opera libretti YU-Lnm, YU-Lsk (j) PIMPINON, / E / VESPETTA, / INTERMEZZI / MUSICALI. / Da rappresentarsi nel nuovissimo / Nella Salla del Palazo Provinciale / in Lubiana, / Nel Carnevale Anno 1740. / Dalla Signora Antonia Bertelli di Bologna, / E dal Signor Giovanni Michieli, di Padua. / PIMPINON, Und / VESPETTA. / In einem Zwischen-Spill aufgefüh-/ret auf dem Land-Hauss-Saal / in Laybach. / Laybach / gedruckt bey Adam Fridrich Reich-/hardt / einer Löbl. Lag. in Crain Buchdr. (k) Cvetko; Škerlj (l) The libretto contains parallel Italian (verse) and German (prose) texts. Only the Italian text, which seems to be based directly or indirectly on that of 1725a, was sung.

30. A production of *Pimpinone* at Brescia, the year unknown, is cited in Troy, p. 152. Weaver and Weaver (p. 275) list a *Pimpinone* (described as a "scherzo drammatico") performed in Florence in 1735 with a libretto remodeled by Francesco Vanneschi and including a third character, Lesbino; the music (lost) was by G. Chinzer.

Notes to the Appendix

1. For instance, *Pimpinone* was performed at S. Cassiano with *Astarto* in autumn 1708 and with *Il falso Tiberino* in carnival 1709. (The Venetian autumn and carnival seasons can be regarded as a single season, since the singers engaged for the first usually remained for the second.) Conversely, a given opera could be paired with different intermezzi on different nights: the above-mentioned production of *Astarto* was also performed with intermezzi for the characters Catulla and Lardone. The lack of a one-to-one relationship between opera and intermezzi even within a single production was another reason for the separate publication of the intermezzi.

2. Antonio Groppo, *Catalogo di tutti i drammi per musica* (Venice, 1745).

3. Gian Carlo Bonlini, *Le glorie della poesia e della musica* (Venice, [1730]).

4. Venice, Biblioteca Nazionale Marciana, Cod. It. VII–2326 (=8263). The Marciana also possesses an anonymous two-volume opera catalog of somewhat later date, Cod. It. VII–1613/4 (=9035–36), in which similar information on intermezzi appears; this manuscript provided Taddeo Wiel with much of the material relating to comic intermezzi found in his *I teatri musicali veneziani del settecento* (Venice, 1897).

5. Groppo *Catalogo di tutti i drammi per musica*, p. 31.

6. Carnival (*carnevale*) was, in Venice and in many other centers, the principal operatic season. In Venice it stretched from 26 December to Shrove Tuesday. When the year of a given carnival season is cited, it must be understood to include the last six days of the preceding year.

Autumn (*autunno*) was a pre-Christmas season, which, in Venice, began in early October with the performance of spoken comedies in certain theaters. Operas were rarely staged in Venice before November, since in October many patrons were absent, enjoying a *villeggiatura* on the mainland.

Primavera was a spring season, and *fiera* was a summer season, which took its name from the fair (*fiera*) with which it coincided.

7. The spelling of these names has been normalized, so that, for example, "Ongarelli" becomes "Ungarelli."

8. As a rule, studies are listed in the bibliography only when they provide information concerning a given production not found in the primary sources.

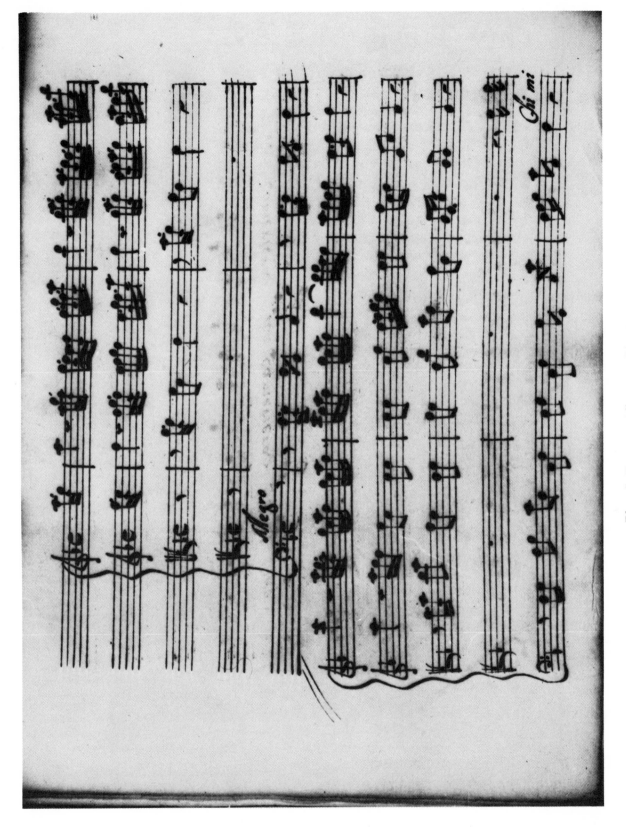

Plate I. Tomaso Albinoni, *Pimpinone.*
First page of music from the score of Intermezzo I, in the hand of Tarquinio Lanciani
preserved in the Diözesan-Bibliothek, Münster.
(Reproduced by permission of the Diözesan-Bibliothek)

INTERMEZZO PRIMO.

Vespetta, e Pimpinone.

Ve. CHi mi vuol? Son cameriera.
Fò di tutto. Pian. M'intendo
Di quel tutto che conviene.
Son dabbene, son sincera:
Non ambisco, non pretendo,
E mi aggiusto al male e al bene. Chi co.
Cerco la mia ventura,
Ma per le vie onorate. Un pò di dote
Farmi vorrei col mio sudor. Ma viene
Il Signor Pimpinone.
Nobil non è, ma ricco a canna, e sciocco.
Che buon Padron saria per me. Vediamo.

Pi. Guai a chi è ricco, guai. Per ogni parte
Ogn'un mi vuol rubar. Più tanta gente
Non voglio in casa mia. Sia benedetto
L'uso delle servette. Una di queste
Per me saria un tesoro... Uh! quì Vespetta.

Ve. Se costui mi accettasse.

Pi. Se volesse costei.

a 2 Seco pur volontier mi aggiusterei.

Pi. Vespettina gentil, come si sta.

Ve. Vossignoria illustrissima perdoni.
Io non l'avea veduta in verità.

Pi. Che belle riverenze.

Ve. Dal maestro di ballo
Ch'insegna ov'io serviva, io l'ho imparate.

Pi. Gran Dama la Padrona esser dovea.

Ve. Che gran Dama? oggidì l'uso non falla.
Adesso il mi la sol, il la la la la la.
Troppo è comune. Ognuna canta, e balla.

Pi. A che giova, a che serve un tal diletto?

A 2   Ve. Se

Plate II. Tomaso Albinoni, *Pimpinone*.
Opening of Intermezzo I in the first edition of Pietro Pariati's libretto, which was published in Venice in 1708.
(Reproduced by permission of the Civico Museo Bibliografico Musicale, Bologna)

PIMPINONE

Intermezzo I
Vespetta e Pimpinone

[1. ARIA]

2

vuol?   Son ca-me-rie- ra,   son ca- me- rie- ra.   Fo di tut- to.   Pian,

pian   m'in- ten- do Di quel tut- to che con- vie- ne, che con- vie-   ne.

Son dab- be- ne, son sin- ce- ra; Non am-

-bi- sco, no, non pre-ten- do; E m'ag- giu-sto al mal e al be- ne. No, non am-

Da capo

-bis- co, non pre- ten- do; E m'ag- giu-sto al mal e al be- ne.

[2. RECITATIVO]

Vespetta

Cer- co la mia ven- tu- ra, Ma per le vie o- no- ra- te. Un po' di

[Basso]

do- te Far- mi vor- rei col mio su- dor. Ma vie- ne Il si-

sí. Ma l'u- so Di- scol- pa un tal di- fet- to, e vuol che

sia L'a- mor ge- ni_o_in- no- cen- te e biz- zar- ri- a.

Pimpinone

Ma quan- ti ge- ni_ha poi la si- gno- ri- na?

Vespetta

Se dis- si_il mal di

lei, Deg- gio dir an- che_il ben: non n'ha che sei. Ma po- co im- por- ta

ciò. La mia pa- dro- na Di buon oc- chio ta- lor non mi ve-

Pimpinone   Vespetta

-de- a. Che in- gra- ta! Ma per- ché? Per- ché tal- vol- ta,

Co- me a dir sul mat- tin pria d'ac- con- ciar- si, For- se di lei più

Pimpinone

bel- la io le pa- rea. Buo- na co- sa è 'l ser- vir un uo- mo, e

so- lo. Non è co-sí? Pia-ces-se al Ciel! Pa- zien-za. Io tro-va- to l'a-

-vea; ma tan-to brut- to... Brut-to com'io? Che di- ce? Al par d'o-gn'al-tro Su-

-stris- si-ma è u-na gio- ia, un gi- glio, un so- le. (O che ca- re pa- ro- le!)

Or che pen- si di far? Cer- car pa- dro-ne. Lo tro-ve- rai. Ma dí: co- me il vor-

-re- sti? Ver-bi gra-zia... vor- re- i... (Quan- to val l'es-ser bel- lo!) Eb- ben, che di- ci? Il vor-

-rei, co-me a dir... Vos- si-gno- ri- a. Or sen- ti, in ca- sa mia son

so- lo e ric- co E, sen- ti, li- be-ral. Se pur ti̲ è ca- ro,

Mia ca- me-rie- ra a- des- so io ti di- chia- ro. Mi vuol bur-

Pimpinone

-lar. (La mia for-tu- na è fat- ta.) Dam- mi la man. Co-sí un par mio con-

Vespetta   105   Pimpinone

-trat- ta. M'in- chi- no a tan- t'o- nor. Pian! Mi fa ma- le. (È

pur de- li- ca- ti- na.) Or- sú, le chia- vi Pren- di del pan, del

110

vin, del- la di-spen- sa. Piú pen-sie- ri non vo'.

Sí, mia Ve-spet- ta, Io mi ri- po- so in te. Ne ve-drà il frut-to. Gra- zie al

Ciel, que- ste man san far di tut- to. In cit- ta- de, in cam-

-pa- gna A tuo pia- cer far e di-sfar po- tra- i. E'l sa- la- rio? Sa- rà...

quel che vor-ra- i. Un pa- dron piú dab-ben non vi- di ma- i.

[3. DUETTO]

Il- lu-stris- si- mo pa- dron!

-gion.

Mi sen- to tut-to in glo- - ria.

(Af-

-fè mi vien da ri- - de-re.)

Su la man. Qui niun ci os-

Da capo

Fine dell' Intermezzo Primo

Intermezzo II

Pimpinone e Vespetta

[4. RECITATIVO]

Ve- spet- ta, tu la- sciar- mi? Tan- t'è. La mia li-

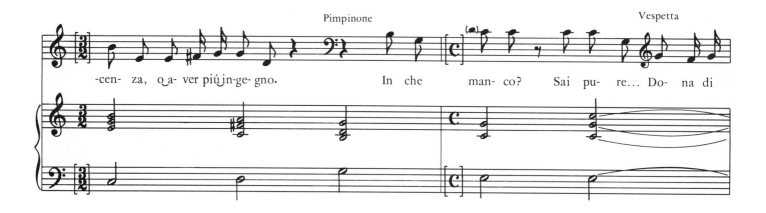

-cen- za, o a- ver piú in-ge- gno. In che man- co? Sai pu- re... Do- na di

qua; pre- sta di là. Si guar- da Me- glio la ro- ba su- a.

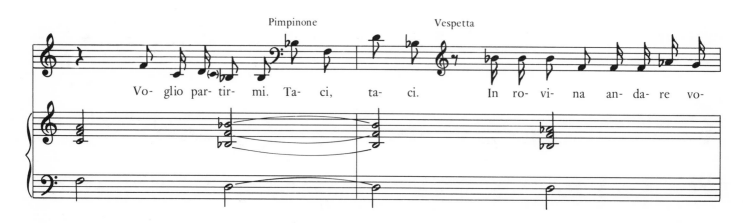

Vo- glio par- tir- mi. Ta- ci, ta- ci. In ro- vi- na an-da- re vo-

di-ci. Pren-di: lo scri-gno_è tuo, ma re-sta me-co.

Vespetta

Per ser-vir- vi l'ac-cet- to. (E- gli_è pur

Pimpinone

cie- co.) Spen- di tu stes- sa, e co-me piú vor- ra- i. Per vo-stro ben,

Vespetta

non per il mio par-la- i.

Pimpinone

(Son fuor d'un bel-l'im- bro- glio.)

Vespetta

(Que-sto_è cer-vel.)

Pimpinone

Da quan-do_in qua le gio- ie? Og- gi me le com-prai con ven-ti scu-di.

Vespetta

Che paz-za va-ni-

[5. ARIA]

lo- ro ve- drai, mio te- so- ro, Che sei di Pim- pi- non, di Pim- pi-

-non _____ la Pim- pi- ni- na, Pim- pi- ni- na.

sei di Pim- pi- non _____ la Pim- pi- ni- na, Pim- pi- ni- na, che

sei di Pim- pi- non _____ la Pim- pi- ni- na, Pim- pi- ni- na.

6

Ti ver- go-gni? Che pen- si? Che fai? Guar- da, guar- da, e guar-dan- do sa-

-prai Ch'il mi- o pre- sen- te a- mor è_____ Ve-spet-ti-

-na, ch'il_mio pre- sen- te a- mor_____ è Ve-spet-ti- na, Ve-spet-ti- na.

Da capo

[6. RECITATIVO]

Vespetta

Ta- ce- te. Ah, trop-po an-ch'i- o... Non vo' dir al- tro. Vi ser-vo an-

[Basso]

Pimpinone

Vespetta

-cor per qual-che gior- no, e poi... Se- gui. Che poi? Su, par- la! Ad-

Par- lo_al-la buo-na. Sei ca-me-rie-ra. È ver, per gra-zia vo-stra. E se tu'l

vuoi, ti pos-so far pa-dro-na. (L'ho col-to.) Io sa-rei ben la for-tu-

-na- ta. (Che buo-na cre-a-tu-ra!) A- vrai giu-di- zio?

Mi van- to sen-za_in- gan- no e sen-za vi- zio.

[7. ARIA]

[Allegro]

[Vespetta]

[Basso]

Io non so- no u- na___ di___ quel- le Na- te brut- te e fat- te___

bel- le, E che im-pa- ran sul___ cri- stal- lo A non far un ge- sto in___

fal- lo, A gi- rar guar- di vez- zo- si, E a te- ner la boc-ca a se-

-gno. A gi- rar___ guar- di vez- zo- si, E a te- ner la boc-ca a se-

43

[8. RECITATIVO]

mi- la.   An- dia- mo.   Oh!   Mi scor-da- va il

me- glio. Io non per-met- to   Vi- si- te,   con- ve-nien- ze e com-pli-

Vespetta

Pimpinone

-men- ti.   In- ten- do,   e ub- bi- di- rò.   Lie- to son

Vespetta

i- o.   (Pro- met- to   al suo pia- cer   per fa- re il mi- o.)

[9. DUETTO]

Sten- di, [sten- di] .

(Tan-to

Vespetta
brut- to, no, non v'è al- cun, no, no,

Pimpinone
(Tal bel- lez- za non l'ha nes- su- na, no,

no, no, non v'è al- cun. È pur cot- to il sem- pli- ciot- to. Per a-

no, non l'ha nes- su- na. Per a-

Adagio

Fine dell' Intermezzo Secondo

Intermezzo III
Vespetta e Pimpinone

[10. RECITATIVO]

Vespetta: Io va- do o- ve mi pia- ce. Oh, que- sta è bel- la!

Pimpinone: (Oh, que- sta è brut- ta!) Io vo' sa- per- lo a- des- so.

Vespetta: Deg- gio ren- der ra- gion d'o- gni mio pas- so? Son ma- ri- to.

Vespetta: Hai ra- gion. Io va- do a spas- so. Pimpinone: A spas- so? È que- sto il pat- to? Vespetta: Di-

53

56

[11. ARIA]

So quel che si di- ce, e quel che si fa: "Su- stris- si- ma, [Su- stris- si- ma], co- me si sta?" "Be- ne, be- ne." E poi su- bi- to: "Quel mio ma- ri- to È pur stra- va- gan- te, è

pur in- di- scre- to. Pre- ten- de che in ca- sa io stia tut-to il dí." So

quel che si di- ce, e quel che si fa: "Su- stris- si- ma, [Su- stris- si- ma],

co- me si sta?" "Be- ne, be- ne." E poi su- bi- to: "Quel mio ma-

-ri- to È pur stra- va- gan- te, è pur in- di- scre- to. Pre- ten- de che in ca- sa io stia tut- to il

dí, io stia tut- to il dí."

E l'al- tra ri- spon- de:"Gran be- stia ch'e- gl'è. Pren- de- te, co- ma- re, l'e- sem- pio da

me. Vo- le- va_an- ch'il mi- o. Ma l'ho ben chia- ri- to. Di far a mio mo- do tro-

-va- to_ho_il se- gre- to: S'ei di- ce di no, io di- co di sí. Di

Da capo

far a mio mo- do tro- va- to_ho_il se- gre- to: S'ei di- ce di no, io di- co di sí."

[12. RECITATIVO]

[Pimpinone] Per que-sta vol-ta an-da-te, Ma pre-sto ri-tor-na-te.

Vespetta Del "pre-sto" non m'im-pe-gno. In-fi-no a se-ra. Pimpinone Di Vespetta not-te per le stra-de? Di

gra-zia che qual-cun non mi ru-bas-se. Pimpinone Ma-le-det- to quel

Vespetta dí... Ma-le-dir-mi? In-so-len-te! Pimpinone Ma-le-di- co il do-

-lor ch'ho in que- sto den- te. Va- da, va- da, ma sen- ti... El- la mi

sen- ta. Per l'av- ve- nir vor- rei Piú go- ver- no al- la

ca- sa, e men d'or- go- glio. Ri- spon- do al tuo "vor- rei" con il mio "vo- glio."

Vespetta

Il te- a- tro, la ve- glia, il gio- co, il bal- lo, La vi- si- ta, la

[13. ARIA]

far co- me fan l'al- tre, Ben dan- zar, par- lar fran- ce- se, Star in

ga- la, es- ser cor- te- se, Ma pe- rò con l'o- ne- stà.

Vo-glio far co- me fan l'al- tre, Ben dan-

-zar, par-lar fran-ce-se, Star in ga-la, es-ser cor-te-se, Ma pe-

-rò con l'o-ne-stà. Star in ga-la, es-ser cor-te-se, es-ser cor-

-te- se, Ma pe- rò con l'o- ne- stà.

Vo-glio an-ch'io sa- per co- s'è La ma-ni- glia e la spa-

-di- glia, E chia- mar o l'as- so o il re, Quan- do il pun- to__ mi di-

-rà. E chia- mar o l'as- so o il re, Quan- do il pun- to__ mi di- rà.

[14. RECITATIVO]

Pimpinone

[Basso]

Ma s'io gio- cas- si, e che di- re- sti_al- lo- ra?

Vespetta

Tu'l fa- re- sti per vi- zio, io per di- let- to. Non si

può, non si può! Quel- la ro- ba_è mi- a. (Buo- no.) Se

tan- to spen- des- si in fra- sche- ri- e? Bel ve- der. Sei un

Pimpinone

Vespetta

car- ta, io t'ad- di-man-do a- des- so. (Mi- se- ro me.) Scher-za- i. Ba-

-ston? Vi- ver co- sí piú non si puo- te. O la mia li- ber-

Pimpinone

-ta- de o la mia do- te! (Che deg- gio far? Ne so- no in- na- mo-

Vespetta

-ra- to, Ed es- sa ben lo sa.) Fa quel che bra-mi. (Ho vin-to il pun- to.) Se mai piú mi

[15. DUETTO]

72

Violino 1

Violino 2

Viola

Vespetta

-tà,   vo' li- ber- tà, lo sai, vo' li- ber-   tà,   vo' li- ber-tà.

Pimpinone

va,   va,   va pur, va,   va, va, va, va pur,   va, va, va,

Ritornello

20

va.

-prò rom- per la te- sta.

Mi vor- reb- be, mi vor- reb- be_an- co- ra

que- sta. Chi_ha le mo- gli_in- dia- vo- la- te_in- dia- vo-

Da capo

35

-la- te Pre- sto_af- fè si pen- ti- rà, si pen- ti- rà.

Fine dell' Intermezzo Terzo